NLP Communication & Conscious Leadership

Train your brain to top performance

Camilla Gyllensvan

NLP Trainer

Copyright© Mindboozt Publications 2017

Cover: Maria Malmqvist

Editing and processing: Åsa Bengtsson, Great Little Britain,

www.greatlittlebritain.com

Mindboozt Publications

Kabelgatan 2M

434 37 Kungsbacka

hej@mindbooztpublications.se

www.mindbooztpublications.se

First edition

ISBN: 978-91-88739-19-3

NLP – New Learning Potential

Table of content

1. What is NLP?
2. Methods and models
3. The map is not the reality
4. Communication
5. The meaning of your communication is the response you get
6. The significance of words - Your brain does what you tell it to
7. Conscious, leadership
8. Why should I learn more about NLP?
9. Glossary
10. Testimonials

A few words from the author...

THANK YOU!!

First of all, I would like to thank you for taking the time to read this book. It can really be a valuable investment for you and your future. This book is also valuable to the organizations that get a small part of the profit this book generates. It will help us to make a difference and to contribute to other people's personal growth and development.

The text is an amalgamation or a whole buffet of everything I have learned over the last twenty years, when I have studied, researched and looked for answers to how we (mainly myself) can feel better, be as healthy as we can and at the same time create a life that is as meaningful as it possibly can be. My journey through life has led me to read hundreds of books about personal development, mindfulness, mental training, NLP, psychotherapy, mindset and attitude, to name but a few. Several hours have been spent on education, various courses, lectures and seeing different coaches. Much of this has been amazing and I've learned an incredible amount about myself.

For those of you that don't know very much about NLP or personal development yet, this easy to read a book with fairly uncomplicated language can be the start of something huge, an exciting introduction to help you discover more about yourself and your inner resources. An opportunity to create and shape your life just the way you want it to be, here and now. If you've heard about NLP before and perhaps know a lot about it, then this book will not contain any major new revelations, but I want to invite you to read this with 'new eyes', as if you have just discovered NLP and thereby give yourself the possibility of seeing, hearing and feeling things anew. NLP is not new as such, you will already be aware of and have heard of much of this, but NLP might be a new way of bundling various teachings and methods together. Perhaps you are not utilizing your knowledge in your day to day life. Several of the books I've read have been difficult to get through (and some have been outright boring), lots of them have the same topic, but written in different ways, using different descriptions and entirely different choices of words. Almost as though every book has its own dialect, its own tonality and rhythm, even if the text is more or less the same. What spurred me on to write this book is that I want to share my thoughts, my insights and show you a simple, fun way to learn something new. To me, NLP is just like the sea, the same old sea but never ever identical.

In this text, I have included some of all the different techniques, tools and methods I have used for myself, with clients and in courses I've taught since 2006. One of the main reasons why I wanted to gather this information and write this book was that we often forget the moments when we have felt captured or caught up in our own emotions. The moments when outer circumstances and factors have ruled our life. All the moments when we haven't felt like we are in control of our own life, such as when a relationship is suddenly cut short, or when we lose our job. This sensation can be crippling, numbing and almost swallow you whole. Life becomes empty, meaningless, it is easy to lose your grip on reality and hard to see any light at the end of the tunnel. We can become so totally absorbed by our own problems that we forget that other people have troubles of their own. We might even isolate ourselves, become introvert recluses and stop socializing with other people.

We are not alone. During my working career where I have helped people to grow and develop, there is a whole range of things that we all want to achieve. We want to be successful and enjoy a high quality of life, we want to be involved, feel like we are part of something bigger. We want appreciation and respect and to feel like we are loved. We want to feel alive, not just survive each day as it comes. We want to live in gratitude, not just for ourselves, but also be grateful towards others, because when we experience greater empathy and gratitude towards the people around us, we also strengthen our sense of gratitude towards our own lives, which in turn helps us to reach our own goals and dreams. In order to experience a richer, fuller life, we also need to be able to access all the different parts of our life. By adopting a gracious, grateful approach to life you can give yourself an opportunity to experience more wealth and richness in your life as well as others people's, because when we get to enjoy true joy and blissful happiness, we want to share this experience with others.

By choosing to read this book, you are already contributing to something bigger and something significant. The purpose of this book is not just to guide you and coach you readers, but also provide the same opportunity to people who have not yet had the same chance to develop and reach their full potential.

So once again thank you! I hope this book can help you take the next step towards your dreams and goals. At the same time as you are creating the life you want to lead, it might inspire you to help others too.

Camilla Gyllensvan

1. What is NLP? What exactly is the difference that makes a difference?

Have you ever wondered what makes some people succeed with anything and everything they decide to try their hand at? Or have you ever pondered over why you haven't ended up where you thought you would, or achieved what you had hoped you would? You most probably have, but on the other hand, have you ever noticed that you managed to get all the way to the finishing line and reached your goal without even making much of an effort? How did that happen? What did you actually think, feel or experience? Is that even a difference that makes a difference? Does it really exist?

At the beginning of the 1970s, two Americans asked themselves that very question. They were curious and started working together because they wanted to find out what made certain people score highly or achieve great results in different areas; whether it was having a head for business, being great at sports or succeed in other ways. They started studying different forms of therapy to find out what variations and differences could be seen between the different approaches and if there was a chance this (whatever it was) could be imitated or reproduced. What John Grinder* and Richard Bandler* did was to lay the foundation for

* John Grinder, born 10 January 1940, American author
* Richard Bandler, born 24 February 1950, American author

NLP - Neuro-Linguistic Programming - with the help of several prominent therapists, renowned for their ability to create fantastic results within each of their individual area of expertise. Milton Erickson -hypnotherapist and psychiatrist, Virginia Satir - family therapist, and Fritz Pearls - Gestalt therapist were a few of the chosen ones.

In order to map, study and discover what really was the difference that made a difference, Bandler and Grinder mapped and studied these three people in great depth. Especially when the three case study 'objects' had sessions with their own clients. Something that became obvious during these therapy sessions was that each therapist had their own, unique way of working, a special pattern or method that was repeated over and over again at every client meeting. These patterns differed from therapist to therapist, which corroborates the theory that if we find out how someone thinks, acts or feels in a certain situation, we can also learn how to imitate and use these patterns or recipes to achieve similar, or in some cases even better, results than the original model. These methods and patterns were written down and gathered under the name of NLP - Neuro-Linguistic Programming.

Neuro-Linguistic Programming? What is it and what does it mean?

I have had to answer the question "What does NLP stand for?" so many times and as soon as I have uttered the words neuro-linguistic programming, I have noticed how the person I was talking has glazed over and I have lost them. So I will lay this out and explain things in a different way to you. In a simplified way, you can think of NLP as a user manual for your brain.

N - Neuro = *Our brain*
There is a never-ending information exchange going on inside your brain. It never stops or sleeps. Your brain consists of a load of cells, neurons that through your nervous system are in close contact with each other all the time.

The neurons have offshoots or branched projection, so-called dendrites, that meet, connect and merge. That is how a connection is created between the various nerve cells. For the cells to be able to communicate with one another, each dendrite is smothered in a type of fat called myelin. This myelin enables this communication by being electrically charged, a form of energy that transports the communication from one cell to another, and another, and another. The layer of myelin increases every time you do something, perform a task or think a specific thought, and thereby use a specific cell and dendrite. As a result, this particular connection turns thicker and stronger and eventually we do not even have to reflect or think about the fact that we are using that particular ability or skill. Our behavior has become automatic and we do not even notice doing it. We can use an analogy of a gym. Just like you can exercise a specific muscle, you have exercised that particular dendrite and made it extremely fit, so you do not have to make a conscious effort to think about what to do next. By this point, we have created a habit. Our brain does not distinguish good from bad, right from wrong; it only does what it has been trained to do. It works fast and we do not even reflect on the fact that we make decisions all the time and makes choices in our everyday life. As our habits turn automatic and extremely well-rehearsed, there will be occasions where we miss an opportunity to do something in a different way, because our brain works at such a high speed.

However, if we stop thinking a certain thought or stop doing a certain task, the cell connections grow weaker and the layer of myelin decreases. That means that if you change something in your particular pattern the myelin surrounding that dendrite, connected to that specific thought or action, will grow thinner and eventually disappear altogether.

Our brain dislikes removing a thought, which means that it takes us much longer to refrain from doing something and change our train of thought than it takes to learn something new. To put it simply, we could describe the thoughts you think frequently or your habits and actions you perform easily as wide motorways, while new thoughts and behaviors could be seen as narrow paths in a dense forest, which would need to be used lots of times over a long period time before they are generally accepted as the beaten track. This means it takes slightly longer for the connection to the new behavior to be as strong as the old one and as long as both behaviors exist, we need to keep practicing the new approach or habit. The more we practice and cultivate a behavior, the easier it will be to act in a certain way and the faster we will become at doing it. If we stick with it and keep on practicing, the new way will eventually be just as comfortable as our old ways and we can choose which approach we want to go with.

By actively learning new stuff and change things around, we can start doing things differently and thereby create new results in life. This might sometimes feel easy-peasy and the next second it will be tougher, like two steps forward one step back. Can you remember what it was like when you had to learn how to cycle for the first time, or the first time you jumped in behind the steering wheel of a car and drove off? In the beginning, you really had to concentrate on your every move. Gas, brake, clutch. Or keeping the balance on your bike at the same time as you are pedaling and steering. After a while you became more familiar with the moves, things felt more comfortable and you might even have been able to relax a little. You felt you knew how to use both the clutch and the gas pedal in one smooth movement. You didn't even need to think about it. It had turned into an automatic behavior.

When we do something for the first time and we are not used to it yet, the pattern is the same regardless of the circumstances or the situation. It might be learning a new language, how to communicate better, a new sport, setting new goals or change a behavior. We often need more discipline and motivation to implement a significant change, before we have embedded a new habit. Many of us find it is easier to change when we already have lots of other changes going on in our lives, e.g. a move or change jobs or when we have just had a birthday and passed a specific milestone. Irrespective of which, we might need to motivate ourselves before we have made it into a habit and the behavior has turned into something self-motivating. We do not have to perfect everything, as long as we do something in a different way and keep trying new routes and paths to reach our goal.

Linguistics – *Our language*

As we mentioned in the neuro paragraph, there is a constant flow of communication in your brain and your brain cells communicate via your nervous system. The nervous system sends information to the brain, which then interprets and deciphers all the stimuli via our senses, i.e. what we should see, hear and feel about this information. We can call this a form of external communication. The "automatic" functions of the body, which for instance regulates the heart, our breathing and our inner organs, are controlled by the autonomic nervous system (ANS).

The internal communication is also done via linguistics, i.e. our language. Linguistics is not just the words we say aloud, but also the way we say them, our intonation, pitch and body language. But we will talk more about that later on.

The nervous system needs this language to clarify the interpretation so that we can act or not act upon the information we are given and the linguistics make it easier for us to deal with reality, the world around us. It helps us make out what is real and what is not. This also includes the communication we have with ourselves and the way we talk to ourselves. There are a number of NLP processes specifically designed to help us hear and listen to our own inner dialogue and how we can change it too.

Programming – *Our habits*

We have already talked about automatic habits, behaviors and patterns and us humans base our lives on habits. If you don't believe me, then just take a moment to reflect on what you do over the course of a day; when do you get up, what do you eat for breakfast, what clothes you wear and how do you get to work? Even trivial little details, like which foot you choose to put on the first step in a staircase when you are heading up or down, are down to habits and automatic behavior patterns.

You do these things without even thinking about the fact that they have become automatic. You have learnt how to do it and programmed these habits into your brain, and the human brains are created to hold on to patterns and it does not particularly like to change them in any way. Many of these patterns happen unconsciously and yet we will keep on acting on them until we have received new information that enables us to choose something new and therefore willing to try something else that might work better. We all have the opportunity to change our habits and behaviors, to do something in a different way in order to achieve the results we want. What is needed, however, is the will and attitude to do something in a different way compared to how we usually do it.

Not everyone has been exercising this muscle or has perhaps lacked the will to do this, but most of the people I have met are at least willing to try out new options and give it a whirl.

Micro exercise: Break a habit
Brush your teeth with the "wrong" hand, every day and night over a period of three weeks and notice the difference.

Summary

- NLP stands for Neuro-Linguistic Programming.
- The two founders, John Grinder and Richard Bandler, studied prominent people in various areas in order to map and find the answer to the question 'What is the difference that makes a difference?".
- NLP is about reinforcing what already works well and focus on future progress.
- The more we use a certain train of thought, the stronger and quicker that particular connection will become and after a while that habit/behavior has become automatic.

2. What is NLP good for - models and methods

So what makes NLP so great?

To put it simply, we could say that NLP helps us overcome our mental and learned obstacles by exploring and finding out what they are really about. Because when we get to the bottom of the issue and discover what the crux of the matter really is, we can stop ourselves from continuing in that negative pattern, we can avoid doing something that stops us in one way or another or that makes us feel anxious, worried, fearful. We can also create new ways of getting past these obstacles or act differently in certain situations. We quite simply build new routes and paths for our thoughts and emotions.

When we get rid of things that drain our energy and makes us lose focus of what we are doing that is actually working well, we become aware of what we do, feel or think in these situations. This gives us the opportunity to copy what Bandler and Grinder did, map the successful strategies and apply them in different areas of our life, where our previous strategies have not worked all that well and thereby create a successful formula and new results in other areas too. So this works regardless of whether it is our way of behaving, acting, thinking or feeling about something specific, or whether it is about the way we lead our life, our values or what is important in life. During these years as a coach, I have had many clients that tell me they know what they feel is important in life. Or at least they do early on in the sessions. When we start to talk about this and discuss what they want out of life, there is generally a lot about what they do not want.

Many people are hung up on finding the perfect partner, living in the perfect house, having well-behaved children, getting a good education that will lead to the perfect job and driving a brand new car. We know which abilities, skills, knowledge and behaviors are expected of us and yet we hunt around for even more materialistic things, status and time. We are forever looking for new adrenaline rushes, highs and affirmation, we keep ticking things off our to-do list and we are *still* not satisfied. Because that is just it... If we do not know what we want, how are we supposed to know what it is really about and what actions we have to take care of to get there?

Extract from the book "Alice in Wonderland".
This is the moment when Alice meets the Cheshire cat:

"Which road do I take?" she asked.
"Where do you want to go?" was the cat's response.
"I don't know", Alice answered.
"Then", said the cat, "it doesn't really matter which road you take."

Our thoughts make up and create our world

Research states that an average human being has approximately 65,000 thoughts every day, where only 5% or so are conscious thoughts.

We all create our thoughts based on our experiences. Everything we have learnt, experienced, whatever has happened to us up to this point in time and all the conclusions we have drawn. We then put all these thoughts into context with future events and we recreate them from the memories we have and things we recognize. We learn through and from the people around us, our family, friends, teachers, school, religion, workplace etc.

This process carries on throughout our life and we gather values, beliefs and life rules, both our own and others' and we also interpret these experiences and give them a context. We interpret the information, decipher it and save it in our own memory database.

NLP is a collection of various methods and tools from different teachings and theories. When Bandler and Grinder collected and compiled these methods, they also created models and tools that were easy to use and at the same time so effective they made a real difference. NLP belongs to the positive psychology genre, which works to reinforce everything that is good, healthy and clearly working. NLP is not about removing or avoiding, but about strengthening, boosting and enabling you and other people to function even better. More like an upgraded version of you. As the fundamental parts in this theory are about studying human behavior and the basic beliefs of humans, they decided to coin the acronym NLP.

- **Neuro,** by which we mean nervous system, because NLP is based on the way our mental processes work, i.e. how our thoughts, emotions, behaviors are handled in our brain and senses.
- **Linguistics,** a word relating to language. The language, e.g. words, body language, pitch and intonation, enables us to communicate with ourselves within and the external world all around us.
- **Programming** represents how we have been taught and how we have learnt. Could also be seen as a metaphor that describes us, by using our NLP knowledge, can change our thought patterns, reactions, even our behavior, and thereby reprogramming ourselves.

NLP includes a set of assumptions, also called presuppositions, that could be described as a set of ethical guidelines that form the basis of the different methods. They are not seen as a general, accepted truth, but more of an attitude or approach to oneself and others.

> OK, so approximately 5% of our thoughts are conscious, what about the remaining 95%? What are they?

Early on during our childhood years, we learn things by studying what goes on around us and up to the age of seven we have different development phases that are incredibly important as they affect how we will interpret our surroundings in the future. We then save these stimuli in our memory database. During this period of development, we struggle to separate fact from fiction, right from wrong, true from false. All sensory stimuli that we pick up from the immediate surroundings turn into truths, which might lead to misinterpretations and our conclusions are not always correct. We see, hear and feel like children do as we think, act, behave and interpret the world around us based on what we have learnt as children.

The problems start when we lead our life based on these "truths", which we created when we were kids and we completely ignore whether they are "good" for us or not. The strategies we learnt as children might have worked superbly within our own family or the environment in which we grew up, but could seem completely absurd in the adult world. Our past, or should I say what has worked for us in the past, shapes us. One example might be that every time a child was sad or upset, he or she was given something yummy to nibble on, some candy or ice cream perhaps.

This person grew up and adopted a pattern where it was easier to indulge in some comfort eating than to start digging to get to the bottom of what was really wrong, what that sensation or emotion actually meant. Just as someone, who only got his parents or other's attention when he or she cried, screamed or chucked his things out of the pram, brings this behavior with him into adulthood. A child that was shown love or attention when he or she was quiet, naturally brings this knowledge into their adult circumstances and situations. Now picture two people of different backgrounds get involved in a romantic relationship; one of them screams and shouts to get his way and the other one sits silently, waiting patiently or perhaps just walks away to avoid the argument. Both of them want attention, love and appreciation, but both of them end up sad and disappointed when the result they had hoped to achieve does not materialize. Both of them have learned that their strategy has worked in the past and they only act based on the fact that they have achieved the right results in the past with this behavior.

If they do, they will have an opportunity to discuss things in a way where both parties are both seen and heard and they can present their ideas and wishes without entering into their old patterns. They do not need to act or behave the way they did before. To expect a different result without changing one's own pattern is fruitless.

> Definition of insanity:
> Doing the same thing over and over again
> and expecting a different result.
> Albert Einstein

Thoughts are just thoughts. *Thoughts are nothing but a waste product inside the brain.*

All our thoughts and ponderings about ourselves, our surroundings and our behavior - regardless of the results and what they lead to - they are still *thoughts that we create ourselves.*
Irrespective of whether they are true or not, benefit us or not, they are created from and shaped by our previous experiences. We quite simply use what has worked before. So far. Our unconscious mind, i.e. 95% of our thoughts, does not take into account whether what we are doing is good or bad. The good thing is that we can *choose something else*. We can choose to do differently or quite simply do nothing at all.

It might sometimes feel like we are stuck, like we are not getting anywhere, and that we are kidnapped by our thoughts. That is when NLP can really help us out of a sticky situation. When we are stuck, we are often unaware of what thoughts, emotions or actions make us behave in a certain way. We can utilize the NLP methods and tools to clarify what stops us from progressing. We can pick up on and become aware of these patterns, as well as finding the resources to help us overcome these obstacles and get unstuck, which in turn will make us let go of wrong-doings, injustices and do things differently.
NLP will help you put things into perspective, create understanding, improve communication, simplify, rethink and think afresh. NLP can be used in lots of different areas of your life. It might seem as though NLP is all about performance and results,

but the core or heart in NLP is actually about creating and becoming the best version of yourself, to find your flow and balance in life.

To feel at ease, feel happy, increase our consciousness and presence - all of the things that in fact come naturally to us humans when we are not too busy comparing ourselves to others, obsessed with prestige, praise and/or fame, fill up our to-do-list and think about who is doing the laundry, fetching the kids or what are we having for dinner tonight.

> What will my boss say about this?
> Did I get around to sending that email?
> Did I accept yet another invitation even though my calendar is already full?

All these thoughts create frustration and cost us lots of energy. All these thoughts that might be totally irrelevant or unnecessary, and they are also recycled thoughts that you have already thought before. By that, I mean that most of your 65,000 thoughts per day are unconscious and furthermore they are recycled; either you or people in your surroundings have already thought the same thought. That is because it is impossible to form a new thought without new input from somewhere. Don't believe me? Try thinking a new thought, just by using your mind right now. Hmmm, didn't go all that well, huh? If you instead focus and think about what I just wrote, what happens then? Probably easier to come up with something new now.

We have a tendency to get stuck in a rut, entangled in old patterns of thoughts and we love to brood old wrong-doings like why things panned out in one way or another, I should have..., I ought to..., I need to stop.... etc etc. If we instead adopted the attitude of regardless of what the thought might be, it is only a thought, nothing more. If we could also learn how to let go of these thoughts altogether, we would release so much more energy that we could make great use of elsewhere. If you can imagine that thoughts are like water; sometimes water flows past rapidly and sometimes really slowly. If you put the tip of your finger into the water, it simply parts to form itself around your finger and continues to flow on the other side. You cannot point at a particular spot in the water as it is ever-changing, ever-moving.

The only way to contain water and keep it still is to use some form of receptacle, something that surrounds it, embraces it and holds it steady, like a bottle or a glass. If you use your hand to hold on to water, it keeps on flowing and moving. What you can do is to leave it be, leave it to lead its own life. You can observe the movement, fluctuations and nuances of the water. You don't need to know exactly where your water is, you can simply let it rush past and float on by without your interference.

It works just the same way with thoughts. As I mentioned earlier, thoughts are a waste product from the brain, created and made up by ourselves. You don't have to hold on to all the thoughts involving musts, shoulds, ought-tos and other views. Many of us are completely occupied with pondering about what others think of them.

You can work your way through several of the exercises and processes included in NLP all by yourself, but in order to really understand and experience how effective they are, I recommend that you do them, at least for the first few times, under the supervision of a certified NLP practitioner* or take the step of signing up for a workshop or take a course to make an even bigger impact in your life. A great deal of literature is available, which describes the various NLP exercises and models, so it is not difficult to lay your hands on more information. One important aspect to keep in mind when you engage with a professional NLP Practitioner is that they will guide you through the brambly terrain called exercises, so that you can focus on the actual process itself.

When we are doing these exercises on our own, without any guidance, we might inadvertently try to protect ourselves or refrain from tackling the most important parts, as they might feel scary or create obstacles for us.

If this happens the really strong experiences and results/effects won't materialize in the same way as if we do them together with an NLP Practitioner for instance. It is easy to navigate away from, or not notice, the patterns we have and choose the easiest path.

*NLP Practitioner, Master or Trainer

This is often the path we have always taken, but regardless of what you choose to do or what path you choose to take, you will get a result that differs from the original starting point. The difference will be greater and more substantial if we dare to let go of the process control and let us be guided by someone else, as this will make it easier for us to see, hear and sense what is really going on.

Choose the approach that suits you personally, dare to try new ways and remember everything starts with the first step.

So why should you give NLP a try?

Today there are loads of self-study courses, education programs, teachings on offer from a number of organizations and a whole range of different configurations and designs. NLP is basically nothing new, as I mentioned before this is a collection of different techniques and models that have evidently worked for others before. NLP is about giving you the opportunity to become even more you, an upgraded version of yourself. To see your own resources, assets, abilities and then tap into what is working in your life to be able to do that even more. To dare to be yourself, act based on your values, and live your life to the maximum. Regardless of where you are in life, you can utilize these qualities and knowledge in a more conscious, deliberate way and, as a direct effect of that, create an entirely new results for yourself. Self-development enables us to pick up on the qualities we already have, things that we like about ourselves and others, and use them in a completely new way.

NLP is not just for some people or for a small, select group. No, NLP is there for anyone that wants something more. It is about giving yourself an opportunity to explore exactly what you want more of. Supposing you work with sales and you want to become even better at your job, maybe even the best, NLP can give you new techniques and use tools that lead to better sales and there is an added bonus, as it would also make you a better parent. Or if you are a skilled sportsman today, you could get even better at that at the same time as you become an amazing communicator.

NLP is like a nut, where the shell is formed by the NLP competence and the yummy stuff in the middle, i.e. the nut, is your own knowledge and wisdom. When you apply NLP in your life, with your experience, competence and skills, you will create extraordinary results and the icing on the cake is that you also feel and perform even better.

Development and progress can be done in lots of different ways, so do a bit of soul-searching and find out what you need. Read a book, talk to a friend, go for a walk, meditate or do some mental training. As we have already said in this chapter, there is no absolute truth. You choose your own truth. So the important thing here is that you actually choose something. That you make a decision. And do things differently.

Mental exercise

Our brain cannot process or understand the word *not*. Take the classic example of the pink elephant. If I say to you to "Don't think about a pink elephant", this is probably the only colorful animal bouncing around in your brain right now.

Another good example of this is when adults tell a child "Do not drop the glass!" and what usually happens, well, the glass slips out of the child's hand. If you remove the word *not* in that sentence, it turns into a direct instruction to the brain "Do ~~not~~ drop the glass!" Give it a try! ☺

Summary

- Approximately 65,000 thoughts pass through our mind every day and most of them (95%) are unconscious and actually thoughts we or someone in our surroundings have already thought before.
- Our thoughts are formed by and created out of the experiences we have had up to now and also our values.
- NLP is a bunch of models and methods that help us overcome mental obstacles and fears, in order for us to work in the best possible, optimal way.

3. Presuppositions – The map is not the reality

There is a number of presuppositions within NLP and these are guidelines or central principles that impact our attitude and approach, how we see ourselves and how we view other people's resources and assets. These presuppositions have never been proven in any way, and the interesting thing here is what happens when you apply them in your life and assume and act as though they are true. There are more presuppositions than what we have listed here, and depending on which books and sources you use, you will find several different variations of them.

In this section, we will be looking at what "The map is not the reality" really means, how this map is created, how we filter information on a continuous basis and which three filters the brain uses.

- **The map is not the reality**

This statement refers to how we relate to and react upon our map of reality. In NLP we explore how we might be able to change or transform our map and our view of the world, to accept that our map is not the absolute truth, it is not reality as such, and we also learn to respect other people's maps. We don't have to like or accept other people's view of the world, just respect their thoughts on this.

- **Every behavior has a positive intention**

Humans do the best they can with the resources they have available right now, at this precise moment. Humans are not their actions or behaviors.

Accept everyone they way he or she is and change his/her behavior. What might seem like a negative behavior pattern, is only negative if we don't understand or have knowledge of the ulterior motive, cause or intention.

- **We all have all the resources we need to succeed**

There are no resourceless human beings, just resourceless states. Humans function just perfectly the way they are.

- **There is no such thing as failure, only feedback**

You cannot fail! If something is not working, you need to do something else or tackle the issue in a different or new way.

In order to utilize NLP, we must first and foremost understand how communication works. In the NLP communication model, we can see and create understanding around how we and others create their maps of what is real and what is not.

As you read earlier, your childhood years have shaped you and this is because of the people you have met, experiences you have had and events you have seen, heard or felt. You are unique and so are your experiences and your way of interpreting them. No one else could have had exactly the same experience as you have, thought exactly the same thought as you have in each specific situation or paid attention to the same things you have. This has given you a truly unique *map of reality.* This map is a direct result of everything you have done and seen, your thoughts and your perception of the world.

The map helps you understand and navigate through life, and we can compare them to a pair of glasses through which you observe the external reality around you. Depending on which "color" your glasses have, you will perceive the world around you differently compared to other people.

You will not perceive the world as it really is, but in the way your filters allow you to perceive it.

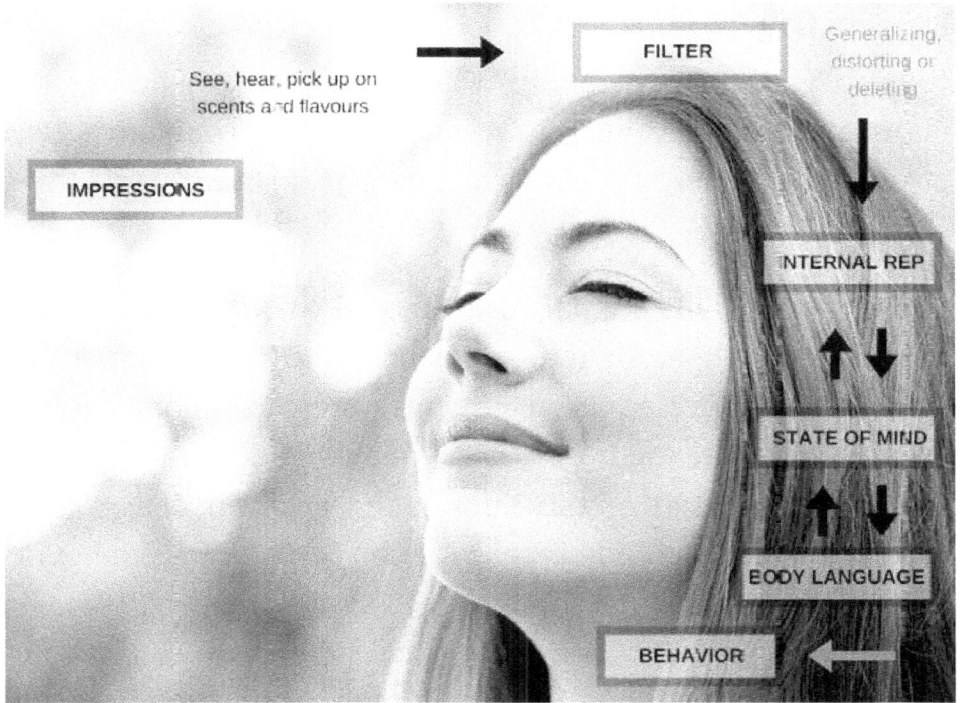

Communication model

In order to for us to understand and relate to our map of the world, we need to translate everything we pick on and everything we have around us. To help us we have our five senses. Sight, hearing, touch/feel, taste, smell. When it comes to communication we usually stick to sight, hearing and touch, which is also reflected in our language and our choice of words, but more about that later on. Taste and smell are also important, but communication is mostly linked to sight, hearing and touch, so we will ignore taste and smell for now.

External event

Our senses make us aware of what is going on around us. New information keeps coming at us and there is a continuous flow presented to us through our sight, hearing and touch.

The external events are perceived and taken in as we see, hear, sense or get a feel for the experience. The sensory input and stimuli are transported via our nervous system to our brain, where some form of filtering takes place. Your conscious brain can only handle a small part of this information and you only register certain selected, limited parts. Our brain receives huge amounts of stimuli on a continuous basis, actually somewhere in the region of 2 Mb per second. We then reduce these to 40 pieces of information per second. These stimuli are not just things presented to us from external sources, but also processes that are going on inside us all the time. If you didn't think about it, you are probably not aware whether one of your limbs is warmer or colder than the others, what it feels like when you are sitting on a chair or standing in a particular way, certain points of sound or light.

This filtering is going on inside us all the time, so that even if we are not specifically aware or conscious of these processes, we need to interpret them and compare them to our memory database. We also need to use our previous experiences and knowledge to determine whether we need to act or react to what is going on around us.

Filtration
We use three filters: Generalization, Distortion & Deletion

The first thing that happens is that we delete or omit. If your brain didn't omit a whole load of information, you would go insane and your brain would overheat. In a simplistic way, we can describe this as though your brain uses your previous experiences and events to be able to remove things that are irrelevant or not important for you. That is why two people can experience the same thing and still describe the event in two completely different ways. If it is important for you to notice differences, you will most probably pick up on everything that is wrong. You might e.g. have a limited perception of what you are capable of achieving or not, and then your brain will automatically discard all feasible solutions that would prove your belief and truth to be incorrect. Your brain cannot focus on negative situations and notice all the positive aspects at the same time.

The next process is distortion. That means that your brain distorts parts of what you observe and note, so that what your brain registers doesn't match what your senses are conveying back to you. We might not care all that much about something, or exaggerate something or reduce the information we get. We ignore or fail to see details and we might convert or reshape them. One example is when we are unable to see that we are ill. Through our childhood years, we are taught that a minor cold is not all that dangerous and nothing to whine about, which might lead to us not spotting when there is something more serious going on in our body. Anorectics might distort their reality to such an extent that they can no longer look at their own reflection in the mirror and see the image that the rest of the people around them can see.

We also have a filter that **generalizes** and this is to help the brain to categorize, classify and rank all the information we are taking in, so that we can find similarities and cope with the vast amount of information that our brain has to cope with all the time. It compares the new information or sensory stimuli to previous events and experiences. One example is that people in the West would generally use chairs to sit on. We therefore "know" that a chair usually has four legs, a seat and a backrest. Similar things can also be classed as chairs even though they are not exactly the same as the chairs we are used to. If the item we are looking at has several qualities/properties that match what we have previously linked to a chair, then we will classify it as something that can be sat upon and we take a seat. In other parts of the world the concept of sitting on chairs might not exist and instead the norm is to sit on the floor or on the ground.

Your everyday life is simplified by this classification and categorization process. You don't have to bother your mind with conscious, active thoughts on whether it is a chair or not, which is great and saves you a lot of time, but this filter can mess things up for us if we evaluate or make that judgment a little bit too quickly. A behavior you notice in someone will be judged from your perspective, based on your map. If someone e.g. does not say hi or does not meet your eye when they meet you in the corridor at work, then you might quickly class them as rude, unpleasant or something along those lines, when in fact the person in question had just been busy with a task or on their way to somewhere and hadn't spotted you. This problem can often occur at workplaces and is one of the things that could result in a conflict or even bullying. You might also be too hard on yourself when you are trying something new for the first time and you fail. Many things in life pan out exactly the way we have assumed they will; we create self-fulfilling prophecies and credos that then become our filters. These beliefs will always come true, i.e. you will always be proven right regardless of whether it is true or not.

Internal representation
After we have filtered all the information, we have created a perception, a view and a reference of the experience - a memory. This memory will now influence, remind and work as a framework for all future information and sensory stimuli.

Mental state & mood
Our mental state will continue to shift throughout the day and the continuous flow of information will affect our mood; happy, sad, tired etc. Past experiences from different situations and events will also influence our state of mind.

Body language
Body and mind is one single system; our state of mind affects our body language and our body language affects our mood! What you feel within will be reflected in our body language. The

interesting thing is that we cannot steer our body language to 100%, which means that we inadvertently give away clues to people around us about how we are doing, what we are feeling and what is actually going on inside us. We are often conscious of our posture, i.e. what others can easily see, but things like muscle tension, gestures, eye movements, pupils and breathing are much more difficult to control. Sometimes even impossible. Take poker players for instance; they often use sunglasses or tinted glasses so stop their opponents from seeing their eyes as they could give something away. Excitement or something we like can enlarge our pupils.

Our state of mind and our body language also influence and affect our surroundings. States are contagious and just by changing our body language we can create a whole new state of mind both within ourselves and in others. So we can actually influence our state of mind with our body language and vice versa, i.e. to use our body language to affect our state of mind.

Behavior

Our behaviors are influenced by our inner representation, our state of mind and our body language, i.e. how we choose to act and treat ourselves and others. It is easy to forget about that and focus on categorizing people depending on what they have done. We get muddled up by putting an equal sign between person and behavior. "He is this or that", but the human being is not the same as his or her behavior. Yet it seems as though we "are" or embody a certain behavior.

The truth is that we can always choose to do differently, go with another option. Our behaviors and body language are just reflecting what is going on inside of us. All our memories and internal representations, our state of mind/mood and body language can be altered, amplified and improved *if we want to make a change*. What we do does not equal what we are.

By becoming aware of our filters and patterns, we can also understand how important it is for us to work with our own, internal communication as well as the external communication with others. Everything and anything can be altered if we want it to. Regardless of what is going on around us, every now and then we are bound to get stuck in negative thoughts, bad things happen and many of these events or incidents are beyond our control. Life goes on all the time and we have no other option but to live with it and deal with it the best we can. It is up to us to change our state of mind and not get stuck in destructive thought patterns, which can take up a lot of time and drain our energy too. It is absolutely OK to go through the entire emotional spectrum from time to time and experience happiness, sadness, anger, frustration, a bad day etc etc, as long as you accept responsibility for this and accept that it is what it is.

Some things, such as mourning, might take longer to work through and might require help from a specialist, but once time has moved on, the events have been worked through and we can no longer influence the situation, yet we still feel that it affects how we are doing, what we are feeling and acting - then we have to do something in a different way. We cannot influence what has already happened, we cannot change the past, but we can choose we do from this day forward and how we tackle things from now on.

Brooding will not help. It has been said that the average figure on brooding is 600 times per incident. When we get stuck in these negative mental spirals, brood over and live by our own credos and chosen truths, we always have a choice. We can choose to stop brooding, just like we can choose to continue. We can choose to feel something else, choose to change our body language or even choose to think other thoughts altogether. This might sound too simple and perhaps a bit provocative. Some people might find it challenging to choose something else and I would like to encourage you to ask for help. If you cannot smash the negative behavior on your own, then do not hesitate to contact a coach, therapist or doctor so that they can break the downward spiral. It is important to let go and move on, accept what has happened, learn from the experience and then make new choices. If you can't get healthier, then choose a state of mind that makes you feel better. We can also use other things and tools to change our state of mind, e.g. music.

Break state - to change the state of mind with the help of body language.

Stand up and stretch your hands and arms up in the air, high up towards the ceiling.

Look up and think of something that makes you really happy.
Breathe all the way down into your stomach and feel the difference when you have that happy thought in your mind.

Stand still in that position for a moment. Then I want you to think about something that makes you sad. Keep the same pose, hands in the air and still smiling.
I want you to say: "I'm depressed."

How did that go??
Not all that easy to feel sad and blue now, huh?
Please take a moment to notice the difference in body language when you feel sad. What do you do, in terms of body language, to feel sad or upset?

So in what way does this relate to my map?

When we have filtered our sensory stimuli and created our own map of the world, the way you perceive your world is highly individual. Your map has been created and shaped throughout your life and is extremely significant for the person you are today. We create our own image of the world and that doesn't mean that what we see, hear and feel match other people's images and maps. Other people have their own unique map and sometimes images and maps might clash between different people. The trick is not to change other people's maps, to just be curious, interested and respect the views of others. We don't have to take other people's maps into our own life and we don't have to even like them, we just need to respect them.

All our experiences, stimuli and sensory input are stored and saved in our memory database and these are our own made-up truths. What is good about all this is that you can always choose to widen your map or choose a different image if you so wish.

Summary

- We interpret external events through our five senses. In the field of communication, sight, hearing and touch/feel are the most important senses. We then filter the sensory stimuli and input via our three filters of generalization, distortion and deletion.
- The stimuli are stored in our memory database as internal representations, our memories, which in turn affect our state of mind and our body language. Or our body language affects our state of mind. These all together create our behaviors and how we treat ourselves and our surroundings.
- We can influence and have an impact on our internal representation, our state of mind, mood and body language just by quite simply choosing to do something different.

4. Communication
You are leaking information, it is impossible for you to "non-communicate".

We are constantly communicating via the stimuli and sensory input we receive, both inner and outer influences. Our brain is having a continuous dialogue with us via our nervous system. All the information that comes to us is perfectly neutral until we decide to interpret it and evaluate. That means whatever sensory input and stimuli the nervous system conveys lack meaning and our brain will react to whichever interpretation you choose to make. The state of mind you are in will be visible in your body language and this will be a tell-tale sign of how you feel and how you are doing. To put it simply, you cannot non-communicate.

When I lecture, most of the audience admits that they thought communication is all about our language, i.e. the words we choose to use and in what context. The truth is that the words are actually not very important at all. According to Ray Birdwhistell's study of communication channels from 1970, these are made up of 55% body language, 38% pitch and intonation and only 7% from words. That means that non-verbal communication actually amounts to a massive 93%.

As we are unable to control all the different aspects of our body language, no matter how much we practice and want to believe we can, tiny changes will happen whether we like it or not. It might be blushing, muscle tension, eye movements and our breathing that leak information. Even if we are totally silent, not using any words at all, we are still communicating.

Perhaps you have heard the saying "*Silence speaks volumes*", i.e. what goes on inside of us will be broadcasted on our exterior in the form of body language and behavior. We are constantly sending out signals to our surroundings, which are then picked up by the people around us and also by ourselves. If we choose to look at it from a different angle, we could say that if only 7% of your communication are words you have to make utterly sure that you pick the perfect word for every situation and sentence, so that it cannot be misinterpreted or misunderstood.

Whose responsibility is it to ensure that the communication reaches its target and achieved what it was supposed to do? Another presupposition in NLP is "*The meaning of the communication is the response you get*" and if we assume that is true, a big part of this responsibility lies with us when we don't manage to get our point across in a way that the counterpart understands. We are not solely responsible of course, but if we learn and practice different communication styles, chances are we would be better at making ourselves understood. If we also learn more about how other people see, hear and feel, we can meet them half-way in their unique style of communication. You are responsible for yourself and your own communication, no one else's.

We, therefore, need to become more aware and learn how to communicate with others. Observe, pick up on things, notice and listen by seeing, hearing and feeling. When we have improved in these areas, we can use what we have noticed and meet others in the best possible way with their words, their pace and their values. If you learn how to communicate in the same way as every unique person does, you will find that everything proves to be so much simpler. Listen carefully and tune into the other person, if you are too fast, make sure to slow down. We need to meet and match the communication style of the other person, not our own and bear in mind that we communicate with our entire body, regardless of whether we use words or just body language.

So how do I know how to communicate with others?

Remember the communication model we described earlier? It explained how we create our own reality, what we perceive as real and true about our surroundings and situation. This model also showed how we, with the help of our senses, create and store our memories, how we create states of being/mind, body language and behavior. In this part of the book, we will go through how all of this is linked to communication and why it is so important to understand how communications work, regardless of whether we are consciously and actively communicating or not.

When we focus on the outer world, we are in what NLP calls "uptime", i.e. when we are fully open to accept and receive sensory stimuli from the world around us. You see what you see: color, shape, details etc. You hear different sounds and sense different emotions. You also register various scents and flavors. When we communicate we rely mostly on our vision, hearing and touch, which is reflected in our language too. We often say that something "looks good", "sounds good" and "feels good". That something tastes or smells good is not usually emphasized or used in our daily expressions and communication pattern, even if they might crop up from time to time. When we talk about our senses in NLP, they are called our representation system.

Communication is the key to great relationships

When we say communication is the key to great relationships, we mean that communication is a way of understanding both yourself and others. It is quite simply the prerequisite when you want to create a bond between various people or build a relationship with yourself. Your language is a big part of this and the way you build up your self-esteem and self-image is important too. By using the spoken word connected to our senses, we can create a bond to others and ourselves too. When we understand ourselves and others trust usually develops over time and this is why communication is vital to all human interactions. More about rapport and how you can build *rapport* with others later on.

Do we speak the same language?

When we know something about how a person a person thinks, which patterns/strategies he or she uses and how he or she stores their information, it is easier to forge a good relationship, understanding and rapport. To be familiar with your own representation system and that of others around you is a valuable tool when it comes to getting to know and understanding oneself and others better. Communication starts in some form or another in our thoughts and we use our body language, voice and choice of words to convey these thoughts, which in turn are made up of and shaped by our collected experiences that are stored in our memory. All this information has once upon a time begun as the kind of signals that the brain gathers via our five senses.

We can all communicate via our vision, hearing and touch, but we tend to use them differently and not the same amount of each. We usually have a primary system we tend to favor, which means that if I primarily register stimuli via my vision and think in images, it will show in the way I talk, i.e. what words I choose to use.

When I spend time with other people that have the same representation system as I do, I will function extremely well, but if I meet someone with a completely different representation system, it will be like we are talking entirely different languages. We will find it tough to connect and get our message across, we would probably feel as though we don't have much in common and that feeling might even niggle a little, be a bit uncomfortable. At work, this can influence a whole office and even make working together as a team really hard and thereby, in the long run, affect the results. Apart from different representation systems, differences in how we behave and act can lead to us (as a group) having trouble reaching our target and getting to the finishing line.

If you want to know more about how you communicate and your style, you can map your behaviors and start to understand your own style of communication as well as how you absorb information. This mapping can, for instance, be done with a DiSC analysis and other similar mapping tools. We will now be taking a closer look at the different representation systems and pay attention to which, out of sight, hearing and touch/emotions, you can see yourself. Which one resonates the strongest with you?

Visual personality - communication via eyesight

When we prefer to communication through sight and have our eyesight as our primary sense, words linked to visual input will come naturally to us. This includes words like look, peek, clear, color and focus.

This type of personality often use detailed descriptions and they are very observant, pick up on lots of details in their surroundings. They also want to see something concrete, e.g. images or someone drawing, they often create pictures inside their mind, use inner visualization.

Visual people are often very upright in their body language, straight back and head up. They often talk with their hands placed higher than eye level, they have fast motions and walk quickly. They draw shallow breaths, in the top half of their chest, and that also makes them speak in a loud and clear tone. Eye movements move diagonally upwards from right to left and they are often looking for information in their memory database, their inner representation.

Visual people can be perceived as aloof, as though they are not always present and engaged. Their eyes dart back and forth in the room, as they are quite simply taking in all the sensory stimuli through their vision. Something might move, a curtain might flap in the breeze or a door might open. They have not stopped paying attention, they just need to "*keep watch*" and observe what is happening in the room. Their focus is still on the counterpart, the person speaking or doing something. This can easily be misconstrued as disinterest or lack of focus. Style of learning for visual people are images, so they like PowerPoint presentations and lots of color. They also like to take notes, even though they might never read those notes ever again. They often have an eidetic memory, also called a photographic memory.

Auditory personality - Communication via hearing

Anyone with their hearing as primary representation system will communicate via sounds and sound input. Auditory people find it easier to use and register words that allude to sounds, e.g. sound, resonate, echo, listen and talk, to name but a few. In order to get going, they love when someone tells them something, when they can hear exactly how they are supposed to do something and it needs to *"sound good"*.

Their posture is more relaxed and less tense than with visual people. They breathe further down into their chest and their pitch is usually somewhat lower. They generally do not talk as fast, but more rhythmical and can sometimes be perceived as melodious. The positioning of their hands is more straight ahead of the person when he/she is talking and the movement and gesticulation are relatively calm. The eye movements are somewhere in the middle, roughly level with the ears, either moving from left to right or vice versa to gather information. They love to tilt their head to the side in order to hear better, but they find too much noise bothersome and they prefer to spend time in calm, quiet surroundings. When learning something, it is important to them to have others tell them things and have the option of listening. Sound recordings work a treat.

Kinesthetic personality - communication via touch and emotions

Communicating through touch or feelings means to use and register words relating to a sensation, for example what it feels like to pat something, touching something or sensing something. The words kinesthetic people use are often descriptive words that refer to the feel of something, e.g. heavy, light, feel, grab hold of, lose, drop, warm, cold etc. They need time before they can make a decision, everything has to *feel just right*, nothing is done on a whim.

Kinesthetic people usually have a relaxed posture and can sit with their legs crossed or sometimes even recline in a very relaxed pose. They take deep, calm breaths and can be perceived as a bit slow. They do not talk with their hands, but generally keep them still on their stomach.

Kinesthetics take their time to feel what is going on inside and conduct an inner dialogue with themselves before they answer, which is why it might seem as though they are not always following the conversation or even understanding it. They need time to reflect and they will not rush the process. When they are learning something new, they need to create a sensation or movement linked to what they are learning.

	VISUAL	AUDITORY	KINESTHETIC
WORDS	-Visual	-Auditory	-Kinesthetic
EYE MOVEMENTS	Top left Top right Scanning	Mid left Mid right	Bottom right Bottom left
HEAD POSITION	Craned neck, Facing skywards	Tilted to the side, "telephone cradling"	Head bowed Slouching posture
VOICE	Fast-paced, High pitch, clear voice	Rhythmical Mid pitch	Slow, deliberate Low pitch, plenty of pauses
BREATHING	In the top half of the chest, fast and shallow	In the middle of the chest Steady pace	Deep down into the belly, slow
GESTURES	Skyward, from chest area and upwards Tense body	Hands kept close to jaw/mouth Head tilted to the side	Hands clasped either lying on the stomach or chest. Rounded shoulders

Eye movements

Every human being uses his or her reference system in a unique way. Each and every one of us has their own strategy for how to structure their experiences. The founders of NLP, Bandler and Grinder, noticed that by observing someone's eye movements you can read how the person is thinking. Not what, but how. We can read and distinguish the process that is going on inside another person when he/she is thinking, i.e. how they work it through and how they take the information in.

We have noticed that eyes move in different ways depending on which of the five senses is most active and that the direction of the gaze also differs. The eye movements serve more functions than that and work as a catalyst to gather information. We do, for instance, gather images from memories when we look skyward and if you do not do this, it is virtually impossible for you to recollect that memory/sensory input. Just like when you are trying to recall a sensation, you need to look down. The movements of the eyes can bring forth or access your inner representation and the direction of your gaze establishes which of the five senses your inner representation is using for information. You can, by studying another person's eye movements, see where their eyes are moving when you are talking to him or her. You need to be very observant, because they can move fast and if you also want to notice where or how your own eyes are darting, you can start focusing on how they move when you think of certain things.

When we look up to the top right, we are using our imagination, we daydream, create goals and fantasize about things that have not yet come true. We look up to the left when we want to think about something that has already happened or something that we remember. When we want to imagine what something sounds like, we look to the right (centered from a height perspective) and when we want to remember how, for instance, our favorite song goes we look to the left. Or indeed what waves crashing onto the shore sounds like, or the voice of a significant other etc.

In order to bring forth a particular sensation or feeling we look down to the left and tune in to that. Then we look to the bottom right to find out how we should relate to this feeling and move the eyes back to the left again to feel what that actually feels like.

Sometimes eye movements can be used to tell whether someone is lying or not and to read a person that well, we need to have lots and lots of training and experience in this field. Many think that if they just stare straight ahead nothing will show, or if we just defocus no one will notice anything about your eyes, but that is simply not true.

Summary

- We communicate with our senses and then primarily through vision/visually, hearing/auditory and touch/kinesthetically.
- We automatically choose to use words that stem from or connect to our preferred reference system.
- Depending on which of our five senses we use will be clearly visible in our body language, will be heard in our choice of words and will be noticed in the way we breathe.
- We all have access to and use all three representation systems but to varying degrees, which leads to us communicating most of the time through the system we feel most comfortable with and most used to. That is why we need to learn how to adapt and adjust to the people we meet in our everyday life, so that our communication is as effective as possible.
- We cannot "non-communicate". As much as 93% of our communication is unconscious and we are leaking information all the time, whether we like it or not.

5. The meaning of your communication is the response you get.

It doesn't matter what you are supposed to achieve, big or small, because you have to communicate in every situation. When we suffer from self-doubt or low self-esteem, it is not uncommon for us to lack faith, lose our nerve and not have the courage to stand up for ourselves and say what we really feel. We have previously shared with you that if a behavior does not work effectively and don't achieve what you had hoped, you need to try something else until you reach your target or goal. When you let this strategy embed within and integrate this approach deep within, everything will work much smoother and easier. Your communication will change immediately and will affect both your verbal as well as your non-verbal communication (body language). How our counterpart reacts to this shows us how our message has been taken in by the other person. This gives us the opportunity to adjust our communication if the counterpart has not understood what we were saying the first time around. As we mentioned previously, scientific studies have proven that human communication consists of three main factors:

- Words 7 %
- Voice 38 %
- Body language 55 %

Even if these numbers cannot be applied to every single situation or context, there is something extremely fascinating in this that is worth taking to heart. Your words are only a small piece in the rest of your communication. By getting better at using your voice and gestures, you can improve your communication significantly. You can also view communication as the process you use to understand the other person's map, or to express your own map. You can use it to explain how you have interpreted the world, i.e. what your map looks like.

Many of today's communication issues occur because we perceive the world in different ways and it would be an understatement to say that there is a variety of different angles and viewpoints out there. This, in turn, evokes a whole spectrum of emotions, thoughts and behaviors which lead to a number of conflicts, marital issues, racial preconceptions and wars.

Should we take a moment to consider this in more depth and detail, it is not all that weird that we could all do with a little bit more humanity and mutual respect. None of us can claim we know the *real and true* reality; we only have our own unique, highly subjective interpretation.

When you communicate with others and the response is not exactly what you had wanted or expected, you might ask yourself whether your communication really reaches its target? Do you really get your message across?

There might also be a risk of misunderstanding yourself and you might not end up where you thought you would and this could, in turn, lead to you missing your own goal post and falling short of your dreams.

RAPPORT - *the quality of our relationships*

Rapport (pronounced rapoor) is a word derived from French and it means 'in sync', connection, especially harmonious or sympathetic relation. Rapport is created when we meet another person in their representation system and their model of the world.

It is the foundation of great communication and can be created on every neurological level. Rapport is created immediately and over time trust and faith will evolve. In this context, rapport means that we create a relationship, a bridge between others and ourselves, which then provides a sense of affinity, understanding and it is all built upon honesty and candor.

Rapport is a prerequisite for effective, well-functioning contact and is one of the most important skills we have as humans. If you look around you, in your everyday surroundings, your work, the grocery store or other locations where people meet and talk to each other, how can you tell whether they have rapport or not? Their communication seems to be flowing, their body language seems to be matching and reflecting one another. People that have rapport could be said to resemble a couple dancing, where they mirror and match each other's moves, gestures and eye contact. When there is complete rapport, all parties are comfortable, feel at ease and have a mutual feeling of understanding. The deeper the rapport goes, the more they match each other. Newborn children learn how to match their surroundings by moving rhythmically to sounds, imitate facial expressions and speech. Rapport creates trust and you can create rapport with anyone you want.

In order to generate rapport, you need to participate in the other person's dance by matching and mirroring his body language, and you need to do this respectfully. By doing this you build a bridge between your view of the world and the other person's view. Matching is not to imitate every movement and gesture, but more about following the pace and rhythm of the other person.

Rapport is something we all do and have been practicing for a long time, even if we are not conscious of it. We are born with this ability to generate rapport. When you sing, clap your hands, laugh or even when you are strolling through the streets of your city and end up falling into step, then you have rapport with others. You can probably think of a number of occasions when you have felt everything is fallen into place, you have clicked with someone and have had an extremely close connection to that person.

Research shows that young children create rapport with their mother by adapting, adjusting and imitating the rhythm and movements of their mother.

One of the keys is therefore to *imitate the people we want to spend time with or be accepted by.*

- Rapport is nothing you have, it is something you create in each separate situation.
- Rapport is not manipulation. A manipulative person might seem to have rapport, but if the person lacks openness, respect and empathy for the counterpart rapport can never materialize.
- Rapport is not the same as friendship. You can have rapport with someone regardless of whether you share the other person's views or whether you like him or not.
- Rapport does not mean you have to agree with the other person. It is possible to share someone else's views, but not have rapport and it is absolutely possible to have rapport without sharing the other person's views.
- Rapport is natural, all human beings are capable of creating rapport.

How do we create rapport?

The starting point for rapport is that all people like to see themselves in others and that makes them like the other person from the word go. Old sayings such as "Birds of a feather" or "Great minds think alike" or "Peas in a pod" spring to mind. This is where the greatest potential is when it comes to effective, efficient communication, which is what rapport is all about actually. If communication is the response you get, then rapport is the ability to receiving and accepting that response.

To give you a few examples:

Try to remember a time when everything was calm and quiet and you felt harmonious and peaceful. Can you think of such an occasion when also you had someone right next to you that made a right racket, chattering away really loudly?

Can you remember your reaction? What did it feel like inside your body?

Or can you remember a time when you were bubbling with happy energy and you were eager to get started on whatever task you had ahead of you, but the other person talked soooo slooowly, seemed so lazy and took far too long to do anything at all?

I bet you felt really frustrated and that you sensed you were not on the same level or even on the same page. You had no rapport. There is, however, no right or wrong. These states of mind or moods only show that people react differently to situations. If you want to become a skilled communicator it is important to remember that you will see the best results if you communicate with people in the way they prefer. Even if you only match their representation system and preferred submodalities for a brief period. Misunderstandings happen all too often as people unconsciously misinterpret each other's submodalities, so the vital building block when it comes to becoming a skilled communicator is to match the person you are talking to.

TO MATCH /FOLLOW

- **Body language**
  Posture, rhythm, pace, movements, gestures, facial expressions and breathing
- **Voice**
  Pace, rhythm, tone, language, intensity, loud, quiet, pitch, dialect, accent
- **Words**
  We use different words and phrases depending on which senses we use the most. Predicates are language references that harmonize with our representation system and the words we choose to use depend on our preferences. Dialect also plays a part here.
- **Values**
  Match the language your audience, do not speak use fancy words just for the sake of it. Be curious about the other person's life, what does he/she believe, what truths to they have and hold dear? To acknowledge means to receive the information, take it in and accept what the other person is saying as well as respecting their views. It does not mean that we like those views or share them.

The simplest, easiest way to match is to follow the other person's physiology, i.e. to imitate the other person's posture, facial expressions, gestures, movements and eye movements. This all takes place without us thinking about it when we communicate with other people, it happens without us being aware of it.

It comes naturally, so try to focus and notice this when you talk to someone. By being present and consciously train to improve your matching skills you will eventually achieve even better rapport. It is also important to point out that you should not exaggerate too much, be discreet to avoid offending or provoking the other person as this could have the opposite effect.

Another effective method of matching is to follow the other person's voice. You can mirror pitch, pace, rhythm, intonation and volume, or even the other person's choice of words. If your counterpart uses some specific words, it could be advantageous to use these in your own sentences too. This is something that happens naturally and unconsciously if you are present and actively tune in to your surroundings. This is also a skill you can train and improve on.

Matching the breathing of your counterpart is also very effective and this is often used in hypnosis. You can do this by breathing in and out at the same time as the other person and fall into their rhythm. This is very discreet and thereby usually very effective too. You can also follow the other person's breathing with a finger or speak with the same pace, which is called alternative matching. We might also match the amount of information, e.g. if someone usually talks in very general terms or broad brush strokes, he might perceive you as dull and boring if you become too detailed. The person that likes details and lots of information, might find you too shallow and find it annoying when you only share "the bigger picture" with him, so it is vital to pick up on the right level of detail too and match correctly.

Common denominators, such as hobbies, background, childhood, birth town etc, make us create a communicative safety net, which is one of the most natural ways of creating rapport. On the other hand, if we notice that we don't have any common denominators, we often give up and finish the call. "We didn't have anything in common anyway". So the more similarities and common denominators we have, the better the circumstances of creating great rapport.

Being on the same wavelength

To calibrate is another word for fine-tuning, to set or focus. In NLP we use calibration as a way of getting to the same page or wavelength. You can compare this to how you set a radio channel, regardless of whether you twiddle little levers or knobs or press buttons to get to another channel, there will be interference and noise between the different channels. Sometimes you might even pick up another channel you had not planned to find. We can compare this to communication that does not quite reach its target, that does not get all the way, because there is interference along the line, which is both frustrating and tiresome. Not to mention how challenging it can be to understand what is the cause of that noise. Whenever you want to generate rapport, you need to start with calibration, setting the right frequency and *start fine-tuning ourselves so that we can meet the other person on the same wavelength.*

So how do we know we have rapport?

- When you change your behavior, the other person automatically follows.
- When you start to notice changes, for instance in the other person's body language.
- Rapport has been created when you perceive you are in harmony with each other and over time trust and understanding will evolve.

Mirror, mirror, mirror and lead

In NLP "pacing and leading" is mentioned, where pacing means that you create rapport by matching, following or mirroring the behavior. Leading means that when you change your behavior the other person follows you, i.e. you take the lead. You cannot lead your counterpart if you do not have rapport.

What we actually do is that we pay attention and note other people's style of communication, i.e. sight, hearing and touch and their body language. What we then do is to imitate their way of speaking, moving, pitch and intonation. If the other person for instance crosses his legs, we could cross our ankles. If our counterpart uses a certain word a lot, we can repeat this word and use this in our sentences too. This will send unconscious signals to the other person and remind him of the similarities between us. We are constantly looking for similarities in other people.

When you have followed or mirrored the other person for a while, you can start changing your body language to see if the other person ends up following you. Note potential differences compared to before and pay attention to whether the person starts imitating you instead. If this happens you have already established good rapport and this is an excellent opportunity to put suggestions across, negotiate a new deal or communicate whatever you want to voice. Your counterpart will most likely follow your lead and say yes.

Trust your intuition

Should you find that the other person does not follow you, or that you have lost your rapport and no longer are on the same wavelength as your counterpart, then simply go back to mirroring his behavior again. Put open questions to him, which will lead you back to rapport and communicate with him if you have any ambiguities or lack of clarity. It is vital to not fall into the trap of mind reading or trying to interpreting the other person's behavior. It might be that you have to communicate in an entirely different way. What actually happens is that we use each other as mirrors, looking at each other's body language, choice of words and behavior. When you mirror my body language I will like it as it reminds me of myself. We get a reminder of what we like about ourselves and it feels like we are a good match, as though we click and are well suited. Just like birds of a feather... we like similarities and resemblance. Take a good look around, many of your characteristics, your qualities and hobbies are probably reflected in your group of friends and acquaintances. This proves the birds of a feather theory. If we like soccer or painting, we will find that other people that like these things are similar to us, even resemble us. We will automatically have unconscious thoughts of resemblance and we will believe that they think and feel the same way we do. This is not a truth, even if the similarities are based on our internal representation and our map of the world.

What happens if/when we lose rapport?

Creating rapport does not take long, it can often be achieved in less than a minute. Sometimes we lose rapport even when we would like to hold onto it. What usually happens is that we feel as though we are not in sync.

It might be that the pitch is altered, the body language or voice change in some way. The easiest approach is to ask whether your counterpart follows what you are saying, at the same time as you go back to mirroring them. Mirror, mirror, mirror and lead.

How can I break rapport?

There can be occasions where we do not want to match nor mirror each other. This might be useful when you want to get away from a conversation, terminate a phone call or such like. You can then choose to stop corresponding to the other person altering your body language, your voice, so that you no longer match him/her.

Rapport is an important part in romances as well as in business relationships. You can use mirroring and matching to generate trust and the person will feel good about you and will have a good inner representation of you. Regardless of what you do for a living, you have the ability to create and maintain rapport with others close to you, regardless of experience or background. Something you guarantee will need to be created in order to create and achieve the result you want. Rapport is generated through matching and mirroring. Rapport is a mutual process of response and respect for one another. The trick with rapport is not to create it, but to maintain it.

In this chapter, we have talked about rapport with others. We often find it easier and quicker to apply NLP onto others, but not on ourselves. NLP mentions having rapport with oneself is to understand and respect one's experiences and we expect ourselves to change with very little practice.

Following oneself in this instance is about being present, here and now, mindful and aware of one's signals, for instance when you are ill, when something does not feel quite right etc. We need to understand and take responsibility for how we feel right now (present state) and what we would like to feel like (desired state). We also need to learn how to act and behave, so that we can feel great and reach the goals we have outlined.

Summary

- Rapport is natural and everyone is capable of creating rapport. We are born with this ability and we can practice, practice, practice to become even better at it.
- Rapport is about building an open and honest relationship. Rapport is a prerequisite if you want to create great communication and long-term relationships. Trust evolves over time.
- You can also use rapport to create a good state of mind. The feedback you get when you communicate is proof of how well you are putting your point across or not. If you reach your counterpart or not.

6. The importance of words - Your brain does whatever you tell it to do

The power in the words I AM

If our truths are good and supporting us in what we want to do and achieve, then that is all great. If you, for example, tell yourself "I have all the resources I need to achieve... (a specific goal)" or "I am everything I need to be to..." it will give you strength and help you reach your desired goal. By stating this sort of message, the person instils a belief in himself and his ability, which will most probably lead to that person achieving what he set out to achieve. It does not mean that it won't be a challenge or won't be tough at times, or even that the person won't need help, but it does mean that the person has a greater faith in himself and in his own abilities, which in turn leads to him thinking that he can solve any problems that may occur and also ask for help if need be.

If we take a different statement, such as "I can't..." or "I won't manage...", it will limit all potential opportunities and possibilities. The person has in this case already made up his mind that the task is impossible. In most cases, the person won't even try to make a change as he has already predetermined that this is not feasible, it simply won't happen. This will also affect the person's state of mind, body language, behavior and the ability to find new solutions. This will then be a fabricated truth and a truth that hinders and limits instead of opening up for new possibilities. Furthermore, it will become a self-fulfilling prophecy.

Of course, we realize that not "everyone" can do "everything". We have certain physiological limitations or cultural differences, which stops us from doing "everything". And that is not the intention or what we are aiming for either. Can we just see what limiting truths and beliefs we carry around with us, as well as which ones are actually helping and supporting us, we have the option of choosing something else. The choice to do things differently. If we explore all our options and trust our own ability to master a specific task, the circumstances will be quite different compared to if we do not. If we can see what this is really about and find out the background or cause of our action, we can experience entirely new results. There is always an expectation of what we would like to achieve. Who I am when I actually live, breathe and do what I want to do in my life vs. leading my life in a way I don't particularly like. When we can spot the obstacles along our route or inner blockages, we can also see what resources we have. The bottom line is that we will always be right, regardless of what we think is achievable or not.

Everything you experience in your life is stored in your brain and when you think of what you have gone through these memories will be recreated in your "internal movie theater". Quite a lot of the original memory is sifted out and you end up only remembering certain parts of what you have experienced. If someone asks what you have experienced, you might only be able to recount a part of the incident. That is also why you might hear two completely different recounts of the same event from two different people, because they have filtered and sifted out different things. We remember what we can relate to and put into some sort of context.

It is impossible for us to remember every experience, everything we see, hear and feel, or all the scents and flavors, all the people you have met, all the different states of mind over the space of a day or all the other things your brain has registered. It is not possible, or even desirable, to give an account of all the sensory input in detail. The important thing is to understand how much that is eliminated from the original event when you or someone else gives their version of it. The words used are not the actual event. That is why we need to ask more questions and gather more information, to prevent us from jumping to the wrong conclusions. Words can never fully describe what is going on around us, words are far removed from what we want to recount, they are just the result of what you have already filtered out and you are therefore only giving your account of the memory you have stored in your brain.

The verbal communication you have access to with your language only reflects what you actually say and think. This is a processed and filtered version of the information you have unconsciously saved in your inner representation system. The remaining memory (raw ingredient) is the information that you have stored, but cannot quite put into words. Just like this text, it is a processed version of hundreds of hours researching and learning, endless google searches and a vast number of hours studying NLP, which I have then sorted and summed up and made the information into my own unique truth.

You can view your conscious and unconscious mind as an iceberg, only the tip is visible above the surface and the main bit of the iceberg is hidden beneath deep beneath the surface. These two parts are constantly communicating with each other through images and moods.

If someone asks you "How are you?", you will ponder for a brief moment, pause to feel or perhaps receive a picture of how you are actually doing, before you answer the person. Often we just respond with "Fine, thanks. Just lots going on at the moment" without even thinking about it. How much have we then deleted, distorted and generalized before we answered?

You can also view your unconscious mind as a well or an ocean, where you can dive down and fetch all sorts of information that you can then communicate to the outside world. Much of what exists in our unconscious mind, which could be detrimental to us, we choose not to communicate to the world around us. We have learnt that we answer in a way the other person expects us to, we won't have an answer what is really going on. If we end up being probed further with questions such as "What do you mean by fine?", "Compared to what?" or "What exactly are you referring to when you say lots going on?", we will automatically change focus and can then recreate distorted, generalized or even deleted information.

The strength in decisions

Everything is on your shoulders, it is all up to you and your decisions. I dare say there is a profound force in a decision and many of us have not grasped how much strength we can draw from our decisions. You might have seen the kind of supermen and women out for whom everything seems to just fall into place, their lives are full of happy tales, their childhood was idyllic, they positively radiate well-being and they are fit and healthy too. Can you think of someone like that? Do you know what kind of person I mean? Then you also know that many of these stories do not finish with a happy ending, many of them end up bored, or stuck with addictions, perhaps a shadow of their former self.

Then we have the opposite. People that have taken a different path and, despite all odds, became successful and lead a happy, fulfilled life. Despite a whole range of setbacks and hardships, they carry on regardless, go through fire and rain and show incredibly strong drive and potential. What separates these people from the rest of us? Admittedly, they have had a tough time and a tortuous path until the day they finally decided that enough was enough. That they did not want it like this anymore. And it is there, at that precise moment, where the real strength and inherent potential rest within each human being. It is at that precise moment, where you no longer will take all the garbage, that you can make a DECISION that can really change your life. A crucial decision. A decision to do things differently.

Decisions are not the same as promises. A decision also differs from what we often say in passing, without actually stopping to pause and contemplate what you are saying. If we look at New Year's resolutions for instance, which is generally something we blurt out at midnight on that particular night and probably only really because the people around you are mumbling something about resolutions and promises. "I should try to lose weight.", "I will start exercising", "I really ought to earn more money" or "I will give up candy as of now". This type of statements is important too, but not at all as powerful as when you make a decision to start or stop something for no other reason than you having decided to do so.

> Only by taking a real decision will you change your life in the direction you want to go.

When you have made a decision, you eliminate other alternatives, you cut off all the other thoughts of doing things in a different way. Simple, right? So why do we not do this more often?

Once again I dare say that we are not sure of or understand the power in decision-making, that we have not had enough opportunity to practice and see what we are really capable of achieving. When you make a proper decision, it is like making an agreement or signing a contract with yourself. You know what you need to do. It becomes clear, perhaps even easy, when this is done and you then find the strength you need to carry out this change.

To carry out and implement this type of transformation or change, it has been said that we need to take three important decisions that affect our behavior and actions.

1. **Setting the target - where do you want to get to and what do you want to achieve?**
2. **Belief - What do you think about yourself and your ability to pull this off?**
3. **Strategy - How are you going to do this?**

So make your mind up! Decision time!
All progress starts with you making a new decision. What will separate this decision from all the others you have made previously and have not been able to stick with, even though you have been perfectly aware that you would have so much better off if you had gone through with them.

> Make a new decision about what you want to change.
> Do it today!

Perhaps you want to break some of your bad habits and swap them for something healthier? Or start doing something in a new way? Get up early to meditate or create more time for yourself? Look for a new job?

Whatever you choose to do, it works like this:
The might force in a small step. The "teeny-tiniest" you can promise yourself and really stick with will make all the difference.

Make two decisions that you are willing to hold on to regardless of what is going on around you. Make a decision you know you can stick with for a long period of time. It does not have to be anything big or grand, the most important thing is to be prepared to keep that promise to yourself irrespective of what is going on around your or within you.

It might be to make your bed every day, stop adding sugar to your coffee or only eating sweets at the weekend and not on weekdays. Choose the "teeny-tiniest" thing you can do that will make a bigger difference to your life in the long run. When we make such a promise to ourselves and prove that we can keep this promise long-term, it builds our "decision-making muscles" and makes them more powerful.

Just like I wrote earlier, we are often untrained since childhood or out of practice when it comes to making crucial decisions in our lives. When we make smaller decisions that we stick to "no matter what", we build this skill and these muscles so that we feel more comfortable with making bigger decision and before you know it, you are making entirely new decisions that demand a lot more of you both to implement, carry out and stick to.

Take a couple of moments and write down two vital decisions you promise yourself to carry out and keep.

1.

2.

Good work! You will succeed!

The next unit is about giving you even more tools that will help you pull this off.

BELIEF, TRUST and your own ability

Apart from there being an immense power in the decision-making process, there is also another force that affects all your decisions. It rules your thoughts, emotions and behavior, well, the whole of your life to be honest. Throughout your life, your decisions will be based on how you interpret what is going on around you. Everything you get to experience will be tinged by your faith and beliefs. To believe is a way of urging your brain to work in a certain way. When I was studying to become a mental trainer, there was one exercise we were supposed to do and it was about increasing or decreasing your heart rate. It is not difficult and this is also the explanation to why people within the voodoo culture can die, just by making your heart stop when you have been given the evil eye. Other examples in psychology show that persons suffering from schizophrenia can affect their own biochemistry, bring about illnesses and even change the color of one's eyes if the person believes he/she is someone else.

Another example that I believe many of us experience in our day to day life is "fridge blindness". Have you ever been asked to fetch the something from the fridge (milk for instance), even though you know for sure there is no milk in the house?

You walk over to the fridge, can't see any milk in there and blurt out "No milk here!". At which point your better half comes over and says "So what's this then?", while grabbing the milk carton that's standing right in front of you. So what made you not see the carton? You simply didn't believe there was any milk in the fridge and because of that belief, that conviction, you couldn't see it even though it was right under your nose.

During our childhood years, our upbringing and throughout our life, we create a notion of how life works and this belief becomes the cornerstone in our life. It will steer everything from how we perceive things, our emotions and feelings, as well as the way we act. Can it really influence my behavior like this? It most definitely can, and it does!

Your conviction or belief has an incredible power over you, not least on how you see yourself. That is why the words we use are so important when we talk about our self-image. Some of you might be using affirmations, a concept that is slightly different from our belief system. Some of the creeds I have used in the past and also used in coaching sessions with my clients over the years are:

- We are not our past.
- The past is not the same as the future.
- There is no such thing as failure, just feedback.
- There is always a solution, I just need to ask the right questions.
- Until today I did not know any better, now I can choose to do things differently.
- I can change my life any time I like, just by making a new decision.

There are of course many others and you might come up with some other creeds that suit you better. These have worked as keys that have helped many people to overcome previous failures, disappointments and hardships, which in turn have lead to them daring to believe in themselves and their own ability again.

The belief we have in ourselves is clearly affecting our whole system. Much of what we believe in has turned into to our own chosen truths about what we can or cannot achieve, what people around us can or cannot achieve. It is also up to you to decide which truths to believe. Faith is incredibly powerful and you need to decide what you want to believe in and what you will achieve in life. Furthermore, your beliefs steer you when it comes to your behavior and how you act in certain situations. The important thing is to become aware of which beliefs help you pull something off, help you achieve your goal and support you in your chosen task. That they fill you with energy and joy and strengthen your faith in yourself. One way to illustrate this is the Circle of Belief (or "you will always be right").

The Circle of Belief is a simple model that shows us a different level of thought-feeling-action*.

*Cognitive psychology states that though-feeling-action work in harmony, i.e. that what we feel like and how we act is very much influenced by our thoughts about ourselves and how we perceive and interpret our surroundings.

Belief

The results in your life tend to confirm your beliefs, which lead to your beliefs growing even stronger. You consequently create or find more proof to support what you think is true.

Your beliefs influence the attitude you have to everything going on in your life. You can reason with your conscious mind, while your unconscious mind takes care of a lot of your automatic belief systems that carries on silently in the background.

Result

Attitude

Everything you do and everything you have around you is a result of choices you have made. Even if you say that you have or don't have an attitude, a result is created regardless.

Your attitude affects your behavior and what actions you choose to take. When you then act, your attitude has already influenced you and steered you in both your behavior and action.

Action

©4LIFEacademyAB

The Circle of Belief is built upon the theory of Belief, Attitude, Action and Result. In short, we can define this as what you believe in gives you a certain attitude, which in turn makes you behave and act in a certain way. In the end, you always get the result you said you would get. You are thereby always proven right!

Let's put it this way, if you believe you will not be able to make yourself understood, or that it will not work the way you want it to, your attitude will be affected and you will probably show this with a statement like "It is not even worth me trying, it won't work anyway" or "No one will understand me anyway", or something along those lines.

This will, in turn, lead to us doing or not doing certain things (so-called actions), such as me not saying what I would actually like to say at a meeting or not saying anything at all. I don't join in when I get invited to a party or a dinner, which leads to me not achieving the results I would like to achieve. I will not attend meetings or informal gatherings, which just gives me even more proof of not having anything to say. This, of course, makes me even more convinced that my belief was correct all along and the self-fulfilling prophecy just keeps on spinning its yarn. I am, by definition, always right.

Your belief influences your attitude and approach to everything that happens in your life. You can reason with your conscious level, while your unconscious level takes care of most of your automatic belief system, which is silently working away in the background. It keeps chugging along regardless of where you start and which direction you happen to be heading in. So how can you utilize this in the best possible way?

Take a moment to think about which truths you choose to believe in right now? Which ones are supporting you and are giving you strength to implement the changes you want to achieve? Perhaps you are thinking to yourself "Well, that's easy for you to say. I have believed in this before and it didn't work out all that well." Two questions that pop into my mind are "How do you know?" and "Did you allow enough time for it to actually work?".

> We often overestimate what we can achieve in a month and underestimate what we can achieve in a year.

We could sometimes use a little bit more patience. Perhaps it hasn't worked before because you have been missing the third part. Your ability to carry out changes is directly linked to your visions and which strategy you use to get where you want to be.

You constantly experience things and situations where you use your different senses to take in information. All this information is stored in your brain, even if it isn't accessible to you at all times. When we create our internal representations and memories we also put a frame around what this memory really is or is not. We create our own truth of the event. Words help us clarify and express what it is all about, but at the same time words can limit us and make us stick to truths that are not actually true.
95 % of our thoughts and behaviors are unconscious and happen automatically. Our thoughts are often reused thoughts from our surroundings, our upbringing, childhood or thoughts that we have already had ourselves. This means we might get stuck in events that happened a long time ago. Things that are no longer relevant and no longer going on as such, but we keep on repeating them in

over and over again in the present moment. We apply the same frame to new events regardless of whether the memories are good for us or not. We relive old injustices, wrongdoings and other memories, which in turn makes us create our experience and perception around it. It becomes a self-fulfilling prophecy. We might say that's just the way he/she is (or I am) and there's nothing to do about it. He/she/I won't change, or rather, you can't teach an old dog new tricks.

> Whether you think you can or you think you can't,
> you're right.
> Henry Ford

Whatever we are focusing on actually grows

We have previously talked about how our emotions affect our thoughts and they also affect how we act, our behavior and body language, but many of us are not aware of the fact that it works the other way around too. By this, we mean that our posture also affects how we are feeling. Body and mind is one system and many people claim that our emotions stem from movement. Your posture affects your way of thinking, your feelings and how you react to what is happening around you. The movement pattern of our bodies also affects our biochemistry, from tough exercise to the simplest of facial expressions.

If you are looking at happy people, what do they look like? What movements are they doing and what are they saying?
If you look at a person that is sad or depressed, what does he/she look like?

Of, if you have suffered from depression, what did you look like and what did you feel like? In order to feel depressed, you also have to carry yourself (your body) in a certain way, am I right?

(Take a peek at the "pink elephant" exercise on page 31 and also at the "hands in the air" exercise on page 42)

What do you need to think about when you stand or sit down? How do you need to hold your shoulders and arms, are they hanging loose or are they taut and tense? Where are you directing your gaze? Downwards? Do you keep your head down, neck bent? Are you sighing? Where do you breathe from, deep down in your belly or shallow breaths at the top of your lungs?

There is a whole science behind *feeling depressed* and it might even demand a certain amount of practice to get there. Most of us know what we need to do and what it feels like, because we might have tried it out for ourselves. It is that precise sensation or perception of an experience that makes us feel that way, which has been used in commercials and movies for a long time. And now things are hotting up and getting more interesting, because scientists are starting to research how our emotions affect us. One observation is that we don't actually smile because we are happy, no, we feel happy because we are smiling. The smile itself affects the biochemistry in our body and that leads to several knock-on-effects such as increased oxygen levels in the blood and also increased blood flow to the brain. You can try this by very simply testing out a few different facial expressions and note how they make you feel.

To make a change is to imagine an "as if" scenario. 'As if' can also help a person that is not quite ready to make the leap, not completely and wholeheartedly, and then he or she can pretend and act as though they are. If I, for example, feel as though I am a bit too reserved in certain situations, I can start by taking a couple of steps forward and act as though I am totally fine and confident. It might involve changing my posture, the way I am standing, the way I gesticulate and how I hold my head. I can study someone I feel radiates self-confidence and moves in a confident way, and then I can model their behavior and the way they move. Sort of acting in a play and behaving 'as if'.

It can start off as tiny little changes, but with time you can start to elaborate more and eventually it won't feel 'as if' anymore, but that you are acting the way you have always done. Our brain is unable to separate true from false, so therefore, something you do often and repeat over and over again soon becomes familiar and comfortable. By that point, it has left an imprint in your brain as a powerful, positive pattern of behavior.

Can I give you a suggestion?

The next time you feel stuck in a problem - do something different, something new. Stand up, jiggle and shake your limbs, perhaps have a little dance and put some music on if you need an additional boost. Stand tall and take a deep breath. Then make a grimace, it doesn't matter what it looks like, but do it properly and put 3 vital questions to yourself (preferably in a funny voice):

- What's the purpose/benefit of this?
- What exactly am I doing?
- Will this problem still matter in 100 years from now?

Did that feel like a slightly uncomfortable, new approach? Good!! When you change your physiology and your goal, you will end up in a different state of mind and that also changes your starting point. By altering your state of mind, you will be able to tackle your original problem in a way that is much more effective and powerful.

Is there anyone close to you, in your surroundings, that move the way you want to? Perhaps a friend or acquaintance? Visualize this person. You don't need to know exactly what this person would do, or how they might act, but you can choose the parts that you think would suit you. You can also envisage a world-famous sports personality that has just won a gold medal, how did they act? What did they do? What was their body language like? What's going through their mind?

Before you continue, I want you to reflect on the change you want

to make. Stand up and focus your entire being and all your thoughts on that goal. Start by *hoping* you will reach that target.
I hope I succeed... I hope I don't fail....
What did that feel like inside your body? How are you standing, what's your posture like? Where is your breathing and where are your shoulders positioned? What's your facial expression? What beliefs and truths will you have when you hope to reach your target? Can you, at this point, see that you will both succeed and that you will not?

Imagine you *doubting* yourself, thinking that you might not succeed. *Really doubting yourself.* You don't need to do that for a very long time before you can start sensing something is going on in your body.
What tension can you feel? What happens to your breathing? Give yourself time to explore what happens inside your body.

And now on to the fun bit!
Be absolutely **confident**, you can succeed!

Envisage your goal and be 100% sure that you can reach it. Take a deep breath and experience with all your senses that you are absolutely sure you will achieve this and make this happen. Stand like a self-confident person would stand. How would you stand if you had no doubts whatsoever that you would achieve your goal? You don't need to hope, you know that you will get there. What posture would you choose if you knew you were right? Take it in, what does it feel like. What happens with your breathing? Your facial expression? What would your gestures be like if you beyond all reasonable doubt knew that you would succeed?

What thoughts are going through your mind? I bet these inner pictures that you are seeing are mostly positive images. What truths are you holding on to? Just imagine feeling like this every day.

Start by finding your positive role models, watch how they move, listen to them and pick up on the words they use, because all these things are important to your personal leadership.

The power of your words

This part of the book is about communication and leadership. Two important components in life. Not only do we need to understand how we can communicate as effectively as possible with people around us, but we also need to communicate in the best possible way with ourselves.

We often practice on ways to "get" others to do what we want them to, we tinker and coax, but it doesn't always work. NLP is the art of understanding oneself and others, but we should always start with ourselves. I.e. how we should understand and lead ourselves in the best possible way. At the start of this book, we mentioned that human communication is made up of 55% body language, 38% tone of voice and only 7% are linked to words

(Birdwhistell's study). Things might be slightly different now as the research dates back a few years now and we have changed the way we communicate, but we will stick with these numbers for now just for the sake of argument.

If words only make up 7 % of our communication, is it reasonable to think that our choice of words is important? That the words we choose to use actually affect how well we communicate, that we make ourselves understood and that we create a relationship in the best possible way?

Words affect us in different ways, just like various colors make us feel certain things, words also affect our emotional state. Images and events pop up in our mind when specific words are used and what's interesting is that we can also feel different things depending on our beliefs and values. A couple of examples could be "good" and "indulge".
"What a good girl you have been" or "Good boy, well done." etc etc.
When you read these sentences above, how do they make you feel? Do they give you positive or negative vibes? Are you that good boy/girl? Do you want to be?
Another word that stirs up a lot of emotions is the word indulge or treat. "Today I will treat myself to a couple of cookies" or "Today I'll indulge in a glass of wine, because I have managed to…."

How do these phrases make you feel? Positive or negative feelings? Is treat or indulge words that make you feel strong?

Some people use treat when they talk about deserving something, e.g. I have been at the gym today and had a really good workout so I will treat myself to a piece of cake. Or am I treating myself to some time off from work? Indulge with a spa visit? These words often seem to be linked to some form of performance or task that has to be done first, so if I don't go to the gym I am not allowed that piece of cake. Just a couple of examples of words that might trigger different emotions in different individuals. Some treat themselves, others enjoy.

This is not about avoiding certain words at all costs. It is about being aware that not everyone has the same understanding of certain words and that some words trigger emotions in the other person you're speaking to, which might not match the feeling you are trying to put across.

The words you use create so much more than just a few letters put together. Imagine standing in the check-out queue at the supermarket. The queue is moving really slowly and you have several fully loaded shopping trolleys ahead of you. This is really dragging on and you are getting stressed. Slowly but surely you're getting closer and soon it will be your turn, but then the person in front of you is slowing down on purpose. You can sense you're about to lose your temper and your patience. It doesn't take long before you are absolutely furious. Yes, really, really angry. In your internal dialogue, you can hear how angry you are with the person in front.

You turn to the person behind and mutter something about how slow this queue is. The person behind you is just looking at you and doesn't say a word.

When you finally get to the till and get to pay you are livid and you tell the cashier that isn't it just ###***### amazing that this should take so long to get served!!

Your whole being is fuming, but what have you actually achieved? Did the queue move faster? Did you get the service you wanted? Was it even good fun?

Think about what you were actually doing just to get achieve that anger. You most probably told yourself things so that you could sense anger simmering inside, am I right?

A long time ago I read somewhere that "If you let your anger show, you expose yourself to your enemies and then they win".

I took that to heart and really stewed on that for a while. Feeling anger is not wrong, but it is important to understand where it comes from. If I am disappointed, sad or perhaps irritated?

Imagine standing in the same queue and instead of being angry, you could try being a bit irritated. What feelings pop up then? How would you act instead? Just think if you next time, instead of being furious and yelling at the cashier, could calmly say "Ah well, that was a bit annoying". Huge difference, right? Try that out and see if it works next time you're doing the weekly grocery shop stuck in a really slow queue. If you think of words like angry, tired, stressed out and feeling down, what emotions do they create inside your body? What do they do to your breathing and your blood pressure? What scenarios and images pop up in your head?

It might sound like the simplest thing to just swap a few words around, but the words we use actually do affect and influence our thoughts. And, as we know, our thoughts affect our senses and how we act. Sure, it might sound too good to be true. Swap one word for another and everything is alright, but the truth is that it really is that simple. Try these out and use "irritated" instead of "angry", "kind of interested" instead of "unmotivated", or "perseverant" instead of "stubborn".

Do you think it might change the way you feel inside? Would it lead to entirely different results in your life? Words trigger emotions, but sadly we don't take that into consideration in our daily lives and we usually don't pay too much attention to *which* words we choose to use. We think even less about how they affect us and how they unconsciously make us act and behave. Imagine this: If someone says you have *misunderstood* something, it would probably trigger a different feeling inside compared to if that person told you that you were *wrong* or you were *lying*. Am I right? It basically means the same thing, but the choice of words is different.

The cool thing about this is that it works the opposite way too. You can reinforce your words with others to make them even more powerful. If someone asks how you are doing, most people would answer "fine". But what would happen if you answered *superb* or *fabulous*? Or if you don't say that you have just read an *interesting* book, but that you were *hooked* by the story? Stirs up quite different emotions, doesn't it?

Phase 1:

This is where you become aware of the words you use on a daily basis, i.e. the ones with negative connotations, and then figure out which words you could replace them with. For example:

- Angry - Irritated
- Stupid - Curious
- Failure - Learning
- Different - Special
- Stubborn - Perseverant

Try it out for yourself!
You will probably think of lots of different words, so I suggest you exercise this regularly. Make it into a routine to write down new words that have popped up through the day and replace them with words that have a more positive vibe.

Now onto phase 2.
Which words give you a great, invigorating emotional boost? Take all these positive words and ensure they make magic happen! Here are a few suggestions, to whet your appetite and get you going:

- Interesting - Fantastic
- Good - Outstanding
- Talented - Genius
- Quick - Real dynamite

- Tasty - Delicious
- Fantastic - Awesome

Make this exercise into your own unique "challenge' and not just because it is a "fun thing" to do. Get stuck in whole-heartedly, not "just because". Are you thinking you would rather not do this? Is it tough to get started? To get off the ground? Carry on reading and I will help you further to make sure you are making progress...

The mystical powers of metaphors

How would you describe your life and surroundings? Which stories do you have about yourself? These statements are metaphors and a metaphor is something we use to describe something and liken it to something else. Metaphors work like symbols and can quickly give us important information. We are constantly using metaphors in our daily life to describe what we are experiencing.

- I'm stuck
- Feels as though I have the whole world on my shoulders
- It is pitch dark / jet black.
- I've hit a dead-end
- Everything is on track
- I was born with a silver spoon in my mouth
- Everything in life has been served to him on a silver platter
- He was born with a silver spoon in his mouth
- I can see light at the end of the tunnel
- Everywhere I look there is a new potential path

Life is fabulous or life is a struggle are both metaphors describing life, but in very different ways. They both give us an image of what that person must be going through at that precise time. What feelings pop up inside of you when you hear/read this? Perhaps the first statement brings happiness & gratitude to mind and the other statement makes you think of battles and misery.

Metaphors are built on our belief system. When you use metaphors to describe the way you feel, you also choose the belief system it is linked to. That is why it is important to contemplate your choice of words very carefully when you are about to describe your experience to yourself and others. Once again this might sound far too simplistic, but well, it really is that simple.

A conversation with a client might sound like this:
- *That's easy for you to say. You don't know what I have gone through in life. I can't see any way out of this.*
- *I walk around with a millstone round my neck. A whole load of injustices that really weigh me.*

To get out of that pickle and take in the right direction, you could use even more metaphors. Examples might be:
- *Let's find a new path or open another door, so that you can move on and get out of this.*
- *Let's get rid of that millstone once and for all. Let's get that weight off your shoulders.*

Another example is to get rid of the burden of musts and shoulds. Note how your shoulders are bouncing back as they are no longer weighed down by an imaginary yoke. Some clients can even breathe a sigh of relief and straighten their backs for the first time in a long time.

So how would you describe your life? Like everything in the garden is nice and rosy? A cool journey or just a game? If your life was to be a cool journey, what would be your chosen mode of transport? Who would you bring with you? Would you have fun? How easy would it be to transport yourself and progress?
Do you think that envisaging your life like this would give you a stronger chance and possibility that you would actually design the life you want to lead? Do you think it is possible that you can achieve whatever you want? Arrange everything just the way you want it to be?

Summary

- Whatever you think, you will always get right
- The words you use will affect you in a positive or negative way
- The thoughts you feel will determine if you reach your goal or not, choose those who strengthen you

7. Conscious leadership

Your brain does exactly what you tell it to do. It pays attention to your own internal communication with yourself.

> "Watch your thoughts, they become words;
> watch your words, they become actions;
> watch your actions, they become habits;
> watch your habits, they become character;
> watch your character, for it becomes your destiny."

Our brain is very simple actually. It hasn't changed all that much over the last 40,000 years and works in much the same way as it did back then. It has a task to fulfil, which is to avoid pain and ensure we have a long life. We have strategies to help us achieve this: flight, fight or sometimes stand absolutely still, glued to a spot. When we lived in caves or on the savannah, these were the survival strategies we learned to master.

If you could hear a rustle in the grass, it was obviously better to react quickly and get out of there fast, regardless of what the threat might be, instead of taking the risk and ending up face to face with a saber-toothed tiger. That is why our brain has been programmed to avoid danger and it is constantly switched on to help us avoid anything that would cause us pain. It might be things like food that could make you sick or other dangers such as a hot stove or hob. How many times have you put your hand onto a hotplate? This usually only happens once and then you will become more careful, to ensure it doesn't happen again.

What your brain does is to stay switched on, always on standby, to protect you against new pain at all costs. That is why I have some clients, who e.g. are scared of dogs as they were bitten at some point during their childhood and still feel uneasy around dogs even though the incident happened several decades ago. Or you have some other memory where you were forced to do something you didn't want to or were put in an awkward situation and you promised yourself you would never ever end up in that situation again.

What happens at that point is that you are giving your brain a direct instruction "I will never do that again" or "I will never eat that again" and then your brain will do everything in its powers to keep you as far away from this chosen object as it possibly can.
So what would happen if you have other negative thoughts? Like "I can't take any more", "My job is so boring", "I just can't cope with anything else going wrong", "I have such a lot on my plate, I'm really stressed out and no one understands my predicament", "I will simply die if things don't improve".

Remember that your brain is programmed to keep you alive for as long as possible. What it now does is to try to understand what causes you pain and make sure you avoid this. Regardless of the consequences, this might have on your behavior. Your brain hears you saying that you cannot cope, that you will die, and then comes to the conclusion that your work can't possibly be good for you. It enters survival mode and cannot possibly allow you to put yourself through this trauma and pain, so the brain will do everything in its power to stop you from going to work, i.e. even making you properly ill so that you have to stay at home.

Does this sound strange? Have you ever muttered to yourself that you really could do with a break, just imagine having a couple of days in bed and just sleep, sleep, sleep?
Your brain listens to you and takes its task of keeping you alive very seriously.
When I took my NLP Trainer certificate, my tutor said to me *"Your immune system is always eavesdropping on what you are saying"*. So whatever you tell yourself is a form of a direct order.

"Oh right, you want to stay at home and not got to work? Just spend time all alone and sleep? I can sort that out! You will get the worst flu you have ever had, so no one will even come to visit you as they don't want to catch what you have."

But was that actually what you wanted? Deep down? Probably not?
If we repeat this pattern over and over again, by thinking "Why did I say yes to doing this/driving here/meeting that person, when I'm actually too tired/don't have the time/don't want to" and "Why does it have to be me hosting that meeting/giving that presentation, when I actually hate speaking publically? I will DO

ANYTHING TO GET OUT OF THIS." your brain will tell you "Ok, I'll sort it out! You won't be able to give that presentation with a splitting headache or severe stomach ache".

This actually works regardless of whether it is positive or negative. As we have said before, your brain doesn't take into consideration whether it is good or bad, right or wrong, healthy or unhealthy. It simply believes what you say and then acts accordingly.

We need to be careful with our thoughts and our internal dialogue, because all our brain wants is to understand us and protect us. For some people, it might not be illness, but might instead be procrastination and delaying important goals and decisions in life.

Some of you might be thinking "Well, easy for you to say. That will not work on me. I have tried this before and that didn't work." Or "Yeah, right! In your dreams."

Others might say "That's great, but I don't have the strength to try it out right now. I don't have the motivation to change my ways at the moment." and that is exactly the point where we should be aware of what's happening.

> First we shape our convictions
> and then our convictions shape us.

Our world tends to reflect the attitude or mindset we have and we see what we expect to see. Our body acts and reacts to the world around us. It will match our mindset and the thoughts we have about ourselves and the world around us.

It really is that simple. Try it out for yourself with this quick exercise.

Stand up and stretch your arm out in front of you, now bring your arm as far back as you can. Look where your fingertips are right now and remember how far you got this time. Then you do the same thing again, but this time you will be able to get your arm even further, about 20% further back. This time I want you to close your eyes and keep them shut throughout this exercise.

Tell yourself "My arm will get even further back this time." Say it aloud. Swing your arm back and envisage being super flexible, your arm and your muscles are super flexible and supple.

Think to yourself that you will definitely get 20% further back than before. I want you to paint an internal image where you can see your arm stretching further and further back.

See how your arm moves backwards, how it easily and smoothly works its way back, further and further back. Now open your eyes and see how much further your arm managed to get this time around. Much further, huh?!

The cool thing is that you can do exactly the same exercise again and tell yourself that this isn't possible, you won't get that far back etc. Then see the difference in results. You telling yourself you can do this vs telling yourself you cannot ☺. It works just the same with reaching your toes, either seated or standing up. Start by doing it once and note how far you got, then close your eyes and sense how you melt closer to your feet, the muscles in your back loosen up and you get closer and closer. Flexible and supple, you can get closer and closer, further and further down.

Cool or cool?! I often do this exercise with my client to show them how powerful our internal communication is; that all our thoughts and words actually matter. There are also mental training exercises related to how we can change our physiology just by thinking different thoughts. These are also techniques that are used in sports, such as weightlifters thinking of "This is easy for me as it is feather light", runners thinking "I'm so fast I run at the speed of lightning'.

Your brain believes everything you say, so make sure you let it serve you in the best possible way. This exercise or experiment simply illustrates how our words affect our thoughts and our body language. There are obviously many other examples too.

When I started coaching clients I worked with groups of people that wanted to lose weight. It ranged from just a few kilos to enormously overweight clients. They were given restrictions and instructions about eating, exercise schedules as well as guidance and coaching. Right at the start many of them were really motivated and eager to lose weight, but as time went on the kilos started disappearing, so did their motivation. There was nothing wrong with the program as such, many of the clients achieved their target weight, continued to eat healthily and exercised regularly. But what separated these people from the ones that failed?

Food is one of our basic needs, if we don't eat we die.
About 40,000 years ago, there were periods of famine where there wasn't much food around. So basically our brain is trying to keep us alive by eating even though we could do with cutting back a bit.
We like some flavors more than others, such as sweetness and saltiness. Let's imagine you have decided to change your lifestyle, you eat a healthy, varied diet, exercise regularly and suddenly you find yourself in a situation where you start sabotaging your weight loss.
That is because you are not explicit enough when you are communicating with your brain. You can communicate in lots of different ways and I will give you two examples of how to do it.

Imagine you are at a party and you have a big table in front of you that is laden with several different dishes and desserts. You walk over to the table and you are just about to take your pick of what to eat when you spot your favorite dish right there.

- Oh, that is so yummy, you think to yourself. But I had decided I would stick to the salad.
- Salad, your brain answers. You don't even like salad. That's nothing but bland, tasteless water. But just look at that favorite dish of yours, doesn't it make your mouth water? It smells delicious.

Your brain is now taking things up a notch and says:
- Oh, go on, take some... a small portion won't matter!
- No, I will eat salad, you think aloud to yourself.

The brain responds:
-Salad?! You won't enjoy it. There is no pleasure in salads. I have never heard you say you think salad is yummy. But look here, there are lots of other delicious dishes here.
- Nope, as I told you I'm on a diet and I will eat the salad.

This dialogue carries on and in the end, you serve yourself some salad, but can't resist a tiny bit of the favorite dish. And then you have some more and then a tiny bit more and eventually you have forgotten your salad and are completely full up on what you should have avoided. Your brain is jubilant.
- What did I say? This is delicious, right!?!!! Have another piece!!

This leads to you feeling bad about not sticking to the diet this time either and the result is usually that you keep on comfort eating. There's no stopping you now, you munch ice cream, chocolate and crisps or whatever else you fancy.
- Eat more ice cream, then you'll be happy again! says the brain. And just like that, in a flash, you're stuck in your old routine and old eating patterns and all of this happens just because you haven't communicated clearly enough with your brain.

Imagine the same situation again, the same party and the same buffet.

- Oh, look at all these delicious dishes! says the brain.
- Yes, you answer, but I choose the salad.
- Salad? your brain exclaims, clearly very surprised.
- Yes, salad! I prefer to feel good, be healthy and I love my current lifestyle. If I stick with salad now, I can eat all those other things some other time.
- But you love eating these things, says the brain.
- Yes, I really do, but I love my ideal weight even more. So I choose to stay healthy and feel fabulous.

Can you see the difference? *I choose to.*

When I tell myself that I am choosing, this sends my body and brain a clear message that I am choosing something else, something better. When we say "I want, I love chocolate" our craving for chocolate grows stronger. If we instead say "I want it, but I mustn't eat that." the whole scenario becomes almost unbearable. If we instead use the words "I do want chocolate, but I don't need it" our craving won't be as strong. By repeating these words, you can reduce your craving and instead think you can buy chocolate another day, some other time. You don't have to stop eating chocolate altogether, you just need to communicate clearly so that the craving disappears. This can also be applied to other areas of your life in your entrepreneurship, your professional life, in relationships and education.

Goals and Setting targets

History has proven time and time again that we can't predict the future. When someone succeeds with something that no one believed was possible, we might say "That was pure luck" or 'The timing was perfect" or something along those lines.

Using Roger Banister as an example, the first man to run the "dream mile" in less than 4 minutes. This was 6 May in 1954 and he achieved the record of 3 minutes 59.4 seconds. The really cool thing about this, apart from successfully achieving something that had previously been perceived as impossible, is that no more than 46 days later John Landley set a new record of 3 minutes 57.9 seconds. Since then, the records have been broken several times and today Hicham El Guerrouj's world record is 3 minutes 43.13 seconds.
*Source: Wikipedia

> The word impossibly cannot possibly be used about the future.
> Lars-Eric Uneståhl

This story doesn't actually describe all the hard work and sweat that Banister had to put in before he could achieve the dream mile. The fact is that many people, currently perceived as successful, definitely were not successful from the word go. What they have in common, however, is that they make sure that they start by setting clear targets. They have taken the crucial decision of becoming the very best in their sport, their profession or in whatever field of their choice. What separated them from others was not that they were born with a special gift or talent, which made them so much better than everyone else. They simply envisaged a very well-defined goal.

There are many talented people out there that want to become number one, but what makes them actually achieve this is that they want this MORE than anyone else does. They are willing to go that extra mile that no one else is willing to go. This is true for every area of your life. You can become the best ever when it comes to relationships, money, your chosen sport or art form. The difference is deciding to go ahead and do it no matter what. To do whatever it takes. To have the courage to fail. To have the courage to take the chance. To really want to reach that target. To become the best, you need to have the courage to fail as well as being scared of it and have plenty of courage. Sadly the fear of disappointment or failure scares many people, which results in them not setting any goals at all. What most people miss altogether is that the hardest part isn't setting the target, it is sticking with it and really going through with it once you have decided what you want to achieve.

Goals should be like magnets, they should boost our energy levels and they should make us excited and enthusiastic. One could say that succeeding is not actually all that important, the important thing is what you learn and experience through the whole process.

When we set a target, it is almost like setting the course for a massive cruise ship. If something changes and the skipper has to modify the course, even if it's only a few degrees, it won't be obvious straight away. But after a day or two, the whole vessel could be completely off course and end up somewhere totally different. The same lesson can be applied in life too; small, fairly insignificant, gradual changes often lead to the greatest of breakthroughs.

> Do you remember the "teeny-tiniest"?
> Doing something every day,
> consistently and continuously?

Success is about doing the very best you can, all the time. Not just every now and then, when you feel like it. It is about developing and constantly striving to improve, truly believing that you are progressing and getting a little bit further, a little bit closer to your goal every single day. You will carry on evolving and growing every day for the rest of your life. Believe in yourself and trust that you will succeed.

Reaching the goal is not a competition in its own right; there is no prize for getting there super quick. Nothing can guarantee quick results, nor does everything have to be done perfectly. When we study successful people, there is a formula for success and that is to break your goals down into smaller chunks. Take big enough steps to suit you and let it take time. Plan your milestones, or intermediate targets, and enjoy your achievement. Celebrate as soon as you have reached your milestone, because this journey should be fun too. ☺

Every long hike starts with a first step. We have a tendency to forget that. All big changes are based on:

- **Setting your target – where you want to go?**
- **Faith - what you think about yourself and your ability?**
- **Strategy - how will you do this?**

So what you do need to take that step? Break the habit, stop altogether or start? What did the ones do, who actually dared? Were they not scared or worried? What made them pick themselves up time and time again, dust themselves off, take the next step and get closer to their goal? They all believed that they deserved success and they were willing to create a better future for themselves. So plot the course of your life, everything is down to you.

Where do you want your life to take you? Don't hang about! Don't wait for another day! Do it now!

How can we exercise our brain?
The difference between positive thinking and positive attitude.

Every morning you have two choices.
You can get out of bed and think:
I am so tired, this will not be a good day. How will I have the strength to carry on if I know already that this day will be rubbish?

> Or you can get up and think:
> This is a perfect day. I feel great and everything will work out a treat today!
> The choice is yours.

There are some things in life that we can't influence or affect, things that happen and things we are subjected to. What we can do, and which is actually within our control, is to choose how we act or react to situations or incidents. Whether we choose to see it as a challenge or something you struggle with. "Positive thinking" is probably one of the best expressions for provoking people. I usually add what I feel is the difference between thinking positively or having a positive attitude.

With a positive mind and thought process, it is easier to spot lovely, happy things to experience, which then gives your inner happiness a boost. Our way of being, actually radiates benevolence and joy, which in turn can lead to success. Our health is affected in a positive way too. When you move, you will be more upright, have a better posture, your voice will be stronger and more powerful, as well as your body language will display much more clearly what we actually feel.

To have a positive attitude is about seeing the positive aspect in various situations, focusing on possibilities, spotting the silver lining in every cloud, to think positively and express yourself in a positive sense. Having this approach and attitude means that positive people are happier and healthier, they feel better overall, which in turn means they generate energy and enthusiasm and this makes them more successful. People with a positive attitude act and approach things differently to others. A negative attitude will not only make you miserable, it will also have the same effect on the people around you, while a positive attitude ensures that people want to spend time with you as so much fun stuff happens when you're around. When you adopt a positive attitude, you spread joy wherever you are and that rubs off and gives others a pleasant, comfortable feeling.

A few years ago now, I worked several summers at a theme park, a really challenging job, but great fun too. When the sun was shining, most of our visitors beamed from ear to ear too, and everything seemed to run pretty smoothly. But whenever there was rain, things were not quite as simple. The visitors were more irritated than usual and our summer staff were grumpier than usual.
The attitude I chose for myself was to think that every day is a Saturday. Why? Because that is generally a day that most of us associate with happy times. Did it help me? Definitely!

Having a mindset that supports us with our goals and dreams is not about positive thinking. The beliefs and convictions we choose to base our reality on don't have to be positive. One of the first steps in conscious leadership is to be aware of the internal dialogue that we have with ourselves.
If you want to become more aware, you can start by taking a piece

of paper and start writing down what you are telling yourself. This is boring/This is no fun/I don't like this/This is an opportunity/What a challenge/I get excited by... etc etc.

Try to avoid analyzing, just write down whatever pops into your head.

When you are aware of which words you use, you can also understand how the brain helps you or makes you topple over in certain situations. When we use words that create pain, the brain will quite simply do a detour to stop us from getting close to that pain. But if we instead say "It doesn't always have to be fun, fun, fun. Others might also find it boring. I choose to eat salad today." your brain will stop connecting these phrases to pain. Rewiring or reprogramming is possible.

Your brain isn't all that complicated, it is just programmed to help you avoid pain and painful situations. Do you like physical exercising, then you just need to tell your body that. Do you like spinach, you need to tell your body that too. Do you like your life and are generally happy with your situation, then say "I love what I do!"

> You and your brain is a team -
> make sure that this team is the bestest team ever!

Allow yourself to soak up new energy, inspiration and motivation so that you can tackle all the potential challenges and achieve your goals and dreams. Your brain likes clarity and when you say "I

117

choose this", it understands exactly what you mean. Don't complicate matters, make it simple, play your favourite tune, create a vision board and have fun.

Exercise

In the last chapter, you were given a couple of exercises linked to words. Replacing words that triggered various feelings. Here's another group of words that you can practice on.

These words might be words you use a lot, but never registered that "people" use them that frequently. Observe yourself throughout a whole day or two, what words do you use and how do these words affect you.

People - I
Try - Have a shot
But - And
Should - Want to
Ought to - Need to

So how does that relate to NLP and conscious leadership?

By utilizing the techniques and the tools available within NLP, you can actually shape your own future and have an effect on the future of others too. When you become aware of your inner potential, of the signals and vibes you transmit and also become aware of the fact that you can choose to act and react to what is happening in the world around you, it is easier to be a positive force and by expressing yourself in certain ways, you can become a strong, ever-increasing positive factor.

There are many specific ways of phrasing things and ways to express yourself that make people around grow. Grow stronger and become an even better version of themselves. Many think NLP is only about "getting people to feel good and be healthy", but that's actually only half the story. If we try to flatter people all the time, give them a boost or try to be extra kind to them, of course, they will feel better for a little while. It serves a purpose for that particular moment, but they will generally notice that these are just empty words and most of the time compliments will not make them progress in the right direction. When NLP was first developed, one of the initial steps was language. The creators Richard Bandler and John Grinder were extremely interested in how the human thought process shapes our language and how we can learn so much by just studying how a person expresses themselves, how they phrase things and what words they use. We can then follow the path into their thought process and change potential negative aspects of their mind.

Conscious leadership is about becoming aware of what is limiting you and how you can get past that; how, if you focus on your troubles and problems, you also constrict your opportunities and possibilities of success. When we bump into problems and failures, the person that overcomes the problem the quickest learns something new from their mistakes and experiences and turns them into something positive, will be the most successful person reaping the biggest rewards.

The first step must be to become aware and conscious and to then change any negative thought patterns you might have. These patterns are evident in your language, your spoken word, how your voice sounds, what phrases you use and most importantly what you choose not to say. Then you can identify the patterns and strategies you have and start using different techniques that will help you notice the issues and start solving them. Restrictive patterns can act as a lock-down for your thoughts and affect your life a great deal. They can affect your self-esteem and self-image and the way you express yourself.

Summary

- Your brain has one task, first and foremost. It is designed to do everything in its power to keep you alive.
- Your brain cannot distinguish right and wrong, true or false.
- Your brain listens to your internal dialogue and it listens attentively to what you are saying.

8. Why should I learn more about NLP?

If you ask me, the answer is extremely simple - Because this is the best thing you could ever do for yourself, your future and the world around you.

NLP – New Learning Potential is an acronym I feel suits this theory better than Neuro-Linguistic Programming. Because regardless of what things have been like up to now, whatever way we have learned things in the past, we can always choose to do things differently when we have new information and wisdom. When NLP is combined with coaching or traditional therapy, it might seem like magic as old obstacles, issues and fears appear to disappear all by themselves. Can it really be that simple? Yes, it can, because when we understand how our mind works and how we can use it to our advantage, we can also break those negative patterns and behaviors. NLP as in New Learning Potential is about studying and learning the things that can have a direct impact on our lives; things that we haven't learned before.

As children, we generally do things without thinking. We don't have a clue about low self-esteem or poor confidence. As babies, we are constantly pampered with plenty of attention and when we are taking our very first steps, most of us are blessed with parents that cheer us on and give us plenty of praise and encouragement. We stand up and fall over, get up again and fall over again, get up again and fall over again. Over and over again. I am absolutely sure that when we toppled over for the fifty-fourth time, we didn't all of a sudden think, "That whole standing-up business really isn't for me".

No, we simply get up onto our feet again and have another go at it, and another and another, until one day we actually master this and can stand on our own two feet. Time for the next challenge, we take our first step and fall over, get up again, take a step and fall over. At this point, we don't surrender either. We don't sit down and think "That whole business of walking just isn't my cup of tea." No, we carry on regardless until one day we nail this too and we can walk by ourselves. Helping us on our journey we have people that laugh with us, support and encourage us to carry on, to not give up. It has been said that people, in general, receive 80% of their overall praise before their third birthday. Whether that has been scientifically proven or not, I cannot say, but it sadly seems feasible as the moments of laughter has decreased significantly in the West over the past 10 years. Throughout our life, we study, observe and model our behavior on our nearest and dearest. So if we learn to handle problems in a certain way and at the same time train our mind and brain too, adopting a certain approach/attitude, this combination will decide how we handle the world around us.

When we then start school, we are actually taught very little about everyday life, i.e. how I handle/build relationships, how I handle

conflicts, set goals and achieve them, or how I can invest in the best possible way and become financially literate. Our timetable might include child studies, which in itself is a good thing but shouldn't we also learn how we can become responsible parents and create healthy, sound relationships? Learn about entrepreneurship and success, as well as how we handle stress and how we can lead a balanced, harmonious, blissful life?
To become a good mathematician I need to study Maths, if I want to become better at languages I need to study languages and linguistics.

If I want to learn more about sound relationships, I need to study that and if I want to become successful, I also need to study success. What happens when I, as an adult, realize that it would've been good for me to learn more about meditation and stress management as my job and situation in life stress me out? Or when I realize that I needed to know more about health and exercise because my current lifestyle and situation won't work in the long run? I don't mean that our schools aren't doing a good job, I just mean that the school of today is incomplete and it certainly has development potential. Several schools have added meditation to their timetable and are actively working on seeing every student and each person's unique potential in order to set relevant targets.

One could say that NLP is an insight into personal, conscious leadership and human success. NLP is based on studying and modelling yourself on people that have already learnt how a person should go about reaching their dream and ideal result. NLP makes you more aware and mindful of what you do when you achieve greatness and how you can increase the behaviors that help you achieve your target.

NLP will provide you with methods, tools and presuppositions that will make you more conscious, more successful, more focused to name but a few of the effects that NLP might have on your life, regardless of which area of your life that you wish to improve and enhance. NLP will give you the ability to sort your perceptions, beliefs, convictions and fears. By improving your perception of the world, yourself, other people, your feelings and behavior and your ability to manage your own future, you actually create just that.... your own future, I mean.

Are you ready for an adventure?

If you really want to delve into the wonderful world of NLP, learn more about it, see, hear and experience, and also become a great communicator, I recommend one of our NLP Practitioner courses, some of which is available online. You can, of course, do your own research, find information online and take various shorter courses in order to practice NLP at a decent level. If you really want to make a change and achieve even better, long-lasting results, I would encourage you to take a supervised course in a physical classroom with classmates and a certified NLP trainer, instead of a self-study course online.

NLP is such a cool journey, no matter if you are studying to become a practitioner or taking part as a tutor. I guarantee that it is an extraordinary experience and you will gain knowledge, information and wisdom that will make a direct impact on your life.

Much of what makes us progress during an NLP course is the work we do with our conscious and unconscious mind, in combination with inward reflection and also sharing insights within the group during the different exercises and processes. When you leave the course and enter your 'real life' again, you have gained lots of knowledge and you have a whole new toolbox of methods, tools and ways to realize yourself, to be present here and now, to move forward and to improve your communication skills. What is crucial, though, is that you find your own path. The path that suits you. NLP is one way, but certainly not the only way.

Pick whatever suits you the best and take to heart what you feel is important of what you have read in this book. Every time you read this text you will probably find something new that you can utilize. Remember that you, and no one else, is responsible for your communication. You now also have the option of scrutinizing and erasing the restrictions and boundaries you have created, the beliefs that no longer support you and instead choose to create what you want to have, do or be. There are often several different solutions to a problem. NLP is not therapy, it is an attitude and approach to life on the whole. Our communication, internal and external, opens our minds to greater things. Remember to spend more time honing your listening skills, listen inwardly with all your senses!

9. GLOSSARY WITH A FEW OF THE MOST COMMON NLP WORDS & PHRASES

Anchoring

Each stimulus that consistently triggers a response or a series of reactions.

For instance: The phone rings, I answer.

Flexibility

The ability to pick and choose between a variety of strategies with the purpose of reaching the goal.

Incongruence

When we are inconsistent, express one view one minute and then change our mind straight away afterwards. Or when there is a conflict in what we say and how we act, like: I speak with a trembling voice even though I am calm and cool as a cucumber.

Intention

Our purpose and aim; the desired result after a specific action.

Internal representations

The set of information we store in our brain with the help of images, sounds, emotions, touch, smell and taste.

Calibration
To be able to recognize another person's state of mind by just gauging their non-verbal signals.

Congruence
Holistic state where all the different parts of a person working n harmony to reach the same goal (body language, pitch, intonation, words, behavior, actions etc).

Body language
Our communication with the world around us consists mainly of gestures. As much as 55% is down to the way we gesticulate and facial expressions etc, then the pitch/intonation accounts for 38% and words only 7%.

Lead
When you change your behaviour while having enough rapport with your counterpart so that he/she actually starts following your behavior.

Match
To mirror or match another person's behavior to achieve or reinforce rapport.

The Meta model
A model that identifies language patterns that obscure the real meaning of a conversation/communication by distorting, deleting or generalizing certain points. Specific questions are used to clarify and challenge vague choice of words/phrases, as well as bringing the chosen topic back to sensory experiences and deep structure.

The Milton model
This is the opposite of the Meta model; to use a very vague language in an imaginative way in order to match another person's experience or perception and thereby create a channel to unconscious resources.

Mismatch
To add various behavioral patterns than your counterpart in order to redirect a meeting or conversation, or to bring it to a close.

Modalities
Our internal representations are Visual, Auditory, Kinesthetic, Olfactory (smell) and Gustatory (taste) - VAKOG.

Modeling
To discover the process of internal representations and behavior that enables someone to carry out a task and reach their goal.

Logical Levels of Change
Scientist Robert Dilts created the concept of logical levels of change where he meant that changes take place on many different levels within our body. Some are only behavioral and others on higher levels such as our identity. His system of six different levels is based on environment, behavior, abilities, beliefs and values, and higher purpose.

Reframing
Changing one's conceptual and/or emotional viewpoint, so that the person can reconsider something in a different light and give it a different meaning.

Perceptual filters
The unique ideas, experiences, beliefs and language that are included in our model of the world. The filters through which we see/perceive the world.

Pacing
To follow or mirror another person's behavior.

Predicates
Sensory-based words that indicate a certain internal representation system such as "crystal clear", i.e. linked to vision.

Presuppositions
General beliefs and attitudes that form the basis of a system. Or In this case, the central principles of NLP.

Rapport
The process of establishing and maintaining a relationship of mutual trust and understanding between two or more people. Conscious and unconscious.

Resourceful states
The combined neurological and physiological experience of feeling resourceful.

Strategies
A set of effective behaviors to achieve your desired result.

Submodalities
Distinctions between each internal representation system, the quality of those internal representations. The smallest components of our thoughts. You can reinforce and change submodalities so that you can achieve other results, such as add more sound, color or light to an event or memory, so that the

feel of this image is improved and thereby affect the way you see yourself.

Timeline
How we store images, sounds and emotions in our past, present and future.

State (of mind)
How you are feeling. The sum of all physical and neurological processes inside an individual at any given moment. Joy, sorrow, anger and self-esteem. Our state of mind affects the way we perceive our experience and abilities.

Eye movement
Eye movements, i.e. the direction we look, indicate which internal representation system that person uses at that particular time (vision, hearing, touch/emotions).

10. Testimonials

So why should you study NLP?
The best thing is to ask the people that have already gone through our NLP courses:

"This NLP course has most of all given me new insight into my own well-being and the way I perceive myself, as well as how I can use this in my line of work."
-Rosita, HR administrator

"Very inspiring and complete U-turn in my mind and understanding of what I am like and how I act and behave. I leave this NLP course as an entirely new version of myself and a new view of what I am capable of."
-Mikael, CEO

"Very informative and inspiring. I feel my newfound self-awareness is very valuable, also the realization that communication takes place on many levels and can be perceived in very different ways by different people."
-Malin, nurse

"The NLP course has been extremely interesting and rewarding. Much of it is actually very logical, but in the past I haven't paid attention, observed or contemplated things the way I do now."
-Johanna, factory worker

"NLP is really powerful. I didn't think I would learn this much in such a short period of time."
-Anna, student

"Informative, educational, challenging, questioning, developing, laughter and tears all rolled into one. I will use this new information, wisdom and knowledge to carry on improving. I will utilize this in my family, with my friends and at work."
-Anu, multipreneur and coach

"STRONG! A course with very concrete models and theories all bound together in a well-functioning context. This will be beneficial both at work, in my private life and also to help others to develop too."
-Thobbe, IT engineer and inspiratory

"NLP has helped me sort out my thoughts after a traffic accident and in my mission to create a loving relationship. Through discussions and practical exercises and processes, I've now achieved new results both in my mind, my attitude and my personal finances."
- Jen, NLP and Recovery coach

"An educational, inspiring new way of thinking that challenges old ideas. Good models, worthwhile exercises that can easily be used in everyday situations."
-Helena, lecturer and coach

"Very worthwhile and an easy setup that helps the learning process along in a positive way. Lots of discussions, sharing ideas and thoughts and exercises that give me exactly what I need."
- Isabell, NLP Master Practitioner & Coach

"The NLP Practitioner and the coaching course have given me tools and hands-on exercises that I can use at home and also in my line of work as an online business coach. I can really recommend 4 Life and I look forward to taking the NLP Master course soon."
- Linda, entrepreneur

"Combining mental training, hypnosis and NLP I have been able to reach great results both in my personal development and also in my chosen sport, freediving. With a clear plan, attractive goals, effective exercises and stronger personal leadership I can reach greater depths."
- Kim, self-employed

"NLP has taught me to distinguish between good and bad memories, emotions from relationships, nurture the good ones and accept the bad ones, but don't let them rule me. I can really recommend NLP, it truly works!"
-Ulla, self-employed

"May sound like a cliché, but the NLP Practitioner course really made me see certain things in a different light. To be able to choose my own state of mind, approach situations with a new set of presuppositions, set bold company targets and find the right strategies to succeed. I can also use NLP when I coach my clients, which makes a huge difference to both the client and me."
- Asa, entrepreneur

Bibliography
An introduction to NLP, Joseph O'Connor
NLP at work, Sue Knight
Unlimited Power, Anthony Robbins
International Community of NLP www.icnlp.se

For more information about courses and coaching, please refer to www.4lifeacademy.se

About the author

Camilla Gyllensvan works with leadership development, coaching and is an author too. She has coached people and held courses in NLP, communication and personal leadership for many years and, nowadays she also lectures internationally. Back in 2012, she started her company 4 LIFE Academy AB, which offers internationally accredited NLP courses, coaching tuition and a range of other services relating to personal development.

Camilla has a holistic approach. As far as she is concerned body and mind are connected and intertwined, so you need to address both in order to achieve optimal results and a more balanced lifestyle regardless of whether it's to do with time, energy, money or relationships. She has developed and published several mental training programs and also written books about personal development. Because her strength is to work with strategies for success that lead to fast, long-lasting change, clients from all over the world want to work with her and gain from her expertise. She usually only needs a handful of sessions with her clients to achieve what other therapies have failed to do, namely the kind of transformation the client wants.

NLP and personal leadership are the cornerstones of Camilla's coaching and she firmly believes all parts of life need to be met. She has clients both in the commercial world of business as well as private individuals, which gives her the opportunity to use her specific areas of expertise to tailor bespoke courses and workshops to suit either individual clients or entire management teams.

With Sweden and the whole world as her office, Camilla really lives and breathes her values and firmly believes her company name to be true, namely 4 LIFE – Leadership is for everyone.

Find out more about Camilla, coaching, lectures, NLP courses and online courses at:
www.camillagyllensvan.com

www.ingramcontent.com/pod-product-compliance
Lightning Source LLC
Chambersburg PA
CBHW081939170426
43202CB00018B/2953